Waynesburg College Library.
Waynesburg, Pa.   15370

D1473903

320.973
                                    M141ℓ

Mace, George
AUTHOR

Locke, Hobbes, and the Federalist
TITLE Papers
119239

320.973   M141ℓ
Mace, George
Locke, Hobbes, and the Federalist Papers
119239

LOCKE, HOBBES, AND THE FEDERALIST PAPERS ☆ AN ESSAY ON THE GENESIS OF THE AMERICAN POLITICAL HERITAGE

BY GEORGE MACE

Southern Illinois University Press
Carbondale and Edwardsville

Feffer & Simons, Inc. London and Amsterdam

Library of Congress Cataloging in Publication Data

Mace, George, 1934–
 Locke, Hobbes, and the Federalist papers.

 Bibliography: p.
 1. Hobbes, Thomas, 1588–1679—Political science.
 2. Locke, John, 1632–1704—Political science.
 3. The Federalist. I. Title.
 JC153.H66M28 1979   320.9'73'04   78-22091
 ISBN 0-8093-0890-8

Copyright © 1979 by Southern Illinois University Press

All rights reserved

Printed in the United States of America

Designed by Richard Hendel

To Martin Diamond and Douglass Adair

Ad astra per aspera

119239

CONTENTS

PREFACE

O F more than passing interest to students of American political heritage and culture is the interface between American constitutional law and American political heritage. The interaction between these two entities is the outgrowth of a political-legal system rooted in a paramount and fundamental law. The ultimate and necessary foundation upon which the system rests is the belief that the Constitution is the supreme expression of the people's will. Since the Constitution gains its authority through the people acting in their constituent capacity, constitutional law is fundamental law embodying the people's determination of the proper extent and division of governing authority.

At the same time, the Constitution does not speak for itself. Some voice must pronounce when the ordinary daily acts of government do not comply with the superior dictates of the fundamental law. Americans, for the most part, have accepted Chief Justice John Marshall's claims in *Marbury* v. *Madison* that the Supreme Court was intended, and by its nature is singularly equipped, to speak as the oracle of the Constitution. There have been periods, however, when the Court's role as constitutional interpreter has been questioned so severely that Supreme Court Justices have been portrayed not as clearly defined and objective spokesmen for the Constitution, but as so many individuals expressing their own personal and group interests. In such circumstances, the Court takes on the appearance of an outrageous oligarchy masquerading in the black robes of constitutional impartiality.

Other groups wishing to say what they believe is or is not constitutional are greeted with even sharper rejection, since they lack the sanction created by time and a tradition of acceptance that is part of the political heritage enjoyed by the Court. But no matter who seeks to answer constitutional questions—whether the Court, other governmental officials, pressure groups, or individual citizens —the problem finally is to determine the intent of the Founding Fathers, the bases of which can be explicated only in terms of our political heritage.

Recurrent in the American political heritage have been diverse and frequently oppositional interpretations of that heritage. Now, in other times and places, there is a continuing assessment of the "birthrights," especially in those instances where "human rights" are pitted against "rights of property." A major purpose of this book is to examine that heritage, focusing upon the basic political values and structures, including our natural rights.

Accordingly, I have conducted a close textual analysis of the political theories of John Locke and Thomas Hobbes and have compared both to the theories of Publius in *The Federalist*.[1] My findings have led me to question the traditional view of Locke's high stature as a political theorist and, consequently, the extent of his influence on the genesis of American political philosophy. Although most commentators consider Locke the champion and Hobbes the foe of democracy, I believe the birthrights in our heritage are Hobbesian, not Lockean. Moreover, in terms of stature, Locke ranks below Hobbes, and Publius is superior to both.

I arrived at this judgment only after a close study of what each considered to be good government. I examined the answers of each to such fundamental questions of political theory as what is man's right or best life? And what is the right ordering of civil society necessary to attain that life. I have measured the answers of Locke, Hobbes, and Publius against the following standard: the right ordering of society seeks to eliminate instability caused by man's nature while at the same time preserving the right to life, liberty, and the pursuit of happiness.

At first glance Publius seems to agree wholly with Locke and totally disagree with Hobbes. We therefore appear to be a Lockean nation but this appearance is greatly misleading. To understand why we are instead a Hobbesian nation, we must look to the theories of human nature, which are the basis of any answer to the questions posed earlier.

Few would deny that the Founding Fathers held a Hobbesian view of human nature as passionate, not reasonable. And while only a small number believe that Locke held a similar view, I think we will see, as we examine Locke's own words, that he, too, believed human nature was grounded in psychological egoism. Locke saw the right ordering of a society of passionate beings as either a "limited" government consisting simply in "majority rule," or "limited" government characterized by an unlimited prerogative. If the right ordering is attained through majority rule, then the problem of human nature can be solved by giving the means of controlling the effects of that nature to those responsible for the problem in the first place. What the majority wants on any issue, at any time, is what is right. That notion leads directly to a tyrannical majority or totalitarian democracy, unless man's nature is reasonable. On the other hand, a prerogative power of the sort Locke favored, although it reflects awareness of man's egoistic nature, is little different from Hobbes's wish for "unlimited monarchy."

Hobbes's answer to the problem obviously reflected his awareness of an egoistic nature of man. He first limited government by establishing a prohibited sphere of action. This area is essentially the area of inalienable rights to life, liberty, and the pursuit of happiness. Hobbes considered monarchy the best form of government, since it offered the greatest protection of those rights; he believed that man acting in his public character would sacrifice the public interest for his private interest whenever the two came into opposition. The answer lay in using private interest to attain the public interest. Since no king could be glorious, famous, or strong if his subjects were weak and poor, monarchy was the obvious system to use in making sure the pursuit of private interest attained the public good. But this is where Hobbes was wrong. Kings can still be rich, powerful, and famous if *most* of the citizens are poor. His means of protecting the libertarian sphere was specious. Nonetheless, Hobbes thought this means, together with stability provided by the arms of monarchy, gave the right order.

Publius saw the shortcomings of the orderings of both Hobbes and Locke. But he also knew the solution to the right ordering of society *did* lay in the attainment of the public interest through the pursuit of private interest. That solution plus the sphere of inalienable rights constitute the major basis of our political heritage. Publius further saw the true means of implementing the solution, which constitutes the genesis of our political heritage: the attainment of the public interest through the pursuit of private interest would occur only in a profoundly democratic society following many interests. One interest, or faction, would, thereby, check another. This can only happen when pluralism is a political fact, and this is the insight no political philosopher before Publius conceived. At the same time, majority rule in democracy would serve to protect the rights of life, liberty, and the pursuit of happiness. This is good democracy, as contradistinguished from Locke's bad democracy. American democracy is good democracy because it contains Publius's means of implementing Hobbes's solution to the problem of attaining the public good.

Insofar as our political heritage may be termed Lockean or Hobbesian, we are certainly more Hobbesian than Lockean. Our political system is not characterized by Locke's unchecked majority rule. Moreover, if the majority is checked it is by the prerogative of a monarch. Such a check constitutes a "will independent of society," which is not part of our heritage. Nor are the ends of our society restricted to the protection of life, liberty, and estate. Locke's "property" is too narrow a category, being only part of a larger, more inclusive end, happiness. And happiness is *the* end of Hobbes's thought. In sum, this book portrays Hobbes as the primary basis of the American political heritage and Publius as the genesis of that heritage.

I wish to convey my appreciation to Professor Herbert W. Schneider who read and criticized the entire manuscript. His quiet and profound questions provoked much thought and understanding. I am also thankful to Professor Kurt Glaser, Professor Gerald Runkle, and Professor Willis Moore. Their valued and valuable suggestions have contributed to much which may be of value within this book.

I also wish to thank my research assistants, Chris Marshall, James Larson, and Ronald Teng. Their questions and contributions are many. I am especially appreciative of Mr. Teng's fine editorial assistance.

For fifteen years of intellectual association with my fellow students in numerous classes in political philosophy I am especially indebted.

I wish to thank Mrs. Sharon Stewart who painstakingly and conscientiously typed the entire manuscript.

To my mentors and colleagues to whom this book is dedicated I shall always be indebted.

For any deficiencies contained herein, I solely bear the responsibility.

Carbondale, Illinois   George Mace
September 1, 1978

LOCKE, HOBBES, AND THE FEDERALIST PAPERS

CHAPTER 1 ☆ THE NATURE OF
THE AMERICAN POLITICAL HERITAGE

PHILOSOPHY is the quest for understanding of the nature of things. Political philosophy is the quest for an understanding of political phenomena. An understanding of the nature of the American political heritage lies in the examination of the political ideas, concepts, and institutions handed down from the past and from American ancestors, which, taken together, constitute answers to the two fundamental questions political philosophy addresses. As Leo Strauss has observed in his *Natural Right and History*, these are: What is man's right or best life? and What is the right or best ordering of society necessary to attain that life? The two major questions of political philosophy necessarily are rooted in presuppositions about human nature, for they carry with them the basic philosophical question: What is man?

One's view of human nature ultimately shapes one's views of a purported right or best life as well as the kind of ordering of society necessary to attain that life. If human nature is believed to be primarily reasonable and good, man's basic propensities tend to be viewed in terms of altruism, cooperation, mutual assistance, and the like. On the other hand, if human nature is viewed as primarily rooted in psychological egoism, the sort of behavior anticipated involves competition, conflict, and other asocial modes of behavior. Clearly, such diverse views of man's nature lead to different beliefs as to what is man's right or best life; they also determine the kind of ordering that must take place in society to attain the given view of man's right or best life.

There have been two primary modes of Western political philosophy. The first is the natural-law mode best typified by classical political philosophers such as Socrates, Plato, Aristotle, Cicero, and Aquinas. Though there were differences among these thinkers concerning whether or not man's end was teleological or eschatological, they agreed that human nature was primarily reasonable or altruistic and that *physis* could be understood only as a process. Being was therefore a process of something becoming what it actually is. Although man's behavior indicated a selfish and unreasonable nature, for example, this was only man as he existed at an immature and undeveloped point on his way toward becoming his mature, reasonable, altruistic, and cooperative self.

Accordingly, the right or best life for man was one lived in a situation allowing and enabling him to develop toward what he was becoming: altruistic, reasonable and cooperative. Since it was his "true" nature to be reasonable, altruistic and cooperative, he was by nature a social and political animal. Man's very nature, then, places him a situation where he will have relations with and among other individuals. His nature places him in a situation restricting and ordering his behavior so mutual relationships can take place. Moreover, nature requires that man live in a situation where the development intended by his nature (*physis*) can occur. Owing to his incomplete nature, man cannot attain his *telos* without the beneficial effects of societal institutions. The right or best ordering of society is that which restricts and orders man's behavior in such fashion as will enable him to attain his reasonable and altruistic *telos*.

Thus there are two significant tenets of the natural-law mode of political philosophy. First, law exists within the framework of nature. It exists because man exists. As soon as there is man, there is law, that which orders and restricts and that which, through such ordering, brings about the societal institutions that will allow and enable man to attain his "true" end, his right or best life. Second, since man's natural condition is to be governed by law, the State similarly exists within the bounds of nature. There is no place for concepts such as social contract and popular sovereignty since the State is not an artificial construct of man.

The result of such tenets is to place man in a subservient position vis-à-vis the state. The state exists to control man and direct his development toward his ultimate end. With such a *raison d'être*, the state necessarily attains a position of prior significance with respect to the individual. Since law is natural, the job of the state is to order relationships as they ought to be in the light of the natural law and the resultant natural order. It is through the discovery of this law that man will attain his end, as determined by the natural order of things. This in turn, of course, requires discovery of that law by those best capable of discerning it. The end of the state to make the individual complete, and the matter of who can best discover what man's true end is, determine who possesses the right to rule within a given society, that is who possesses the right to sovereignty.

In either the natural-law mode or the natural-rights mode of political philosophy, the two fundamental questions lead necessarily to consideration of the basic topics of political philosophy. The first topic is power. Taken simply, power is having the ability or capability to attain ends. In the political context, there are two forms of power: authority and force. Authority consists in the imputation of legitimacy. It carries the notion of *ought* with it, which distinguishes it from sheer coercive physical force. Whereas force can create a government in fact, it cannot produce *just* government since the governing power of the latter must consist in a *rightful* exercise. Whereas man can be forced to perform a certain physical action, force cannot control his will. It is authority that has this capacity, and it is only man's will that obliges him.

When citizens view a government as pursuing a rightful exercise of power, they impute authority to that government by recognizing that the exercise and the government are legitimate. Men *ought* to respect authority, but they have no obligation to respect force. For in any situation where authority enters, man has an option. If there is to be an ought, which is what authority is based upon, there must be choice and consent. Force, on the other hand, consists in the use of physical sanctions or the threat of such sanctions. Force may compel a person to accept acts or commit them, but it cannot bring about political obligation.

Political obligation exists when individuals are persuaded that government and its acts or activities are legitimate. A theory of obligation attempts to delineate the demands of the political role and the propriety in response to those demands, obligations, and duties. Thus it answers the self-addressed questions of both citizen and governmental agent: What should I do? Like authority, obligation carries with it the notion of ought. There are two sources of authority in the natural-law mode. Authority can stem from above or outside the system, as in those instances where divine right exists. It can also stem from within the state, as it did in the view of most of the natural-law theorists who believed there existed certain elites. There were the few who were excellent, the *aristoi*, who could determine man's end and the right or best ordering of society necessary to attain that end better than the many (*demos*). In such a situation, claims to authority are always based in some assertion of superior significance, whether a body of absolute truth as with Aquinas, or superior knowledge or abilities as with Plato. Natural law theorists were elitists.

The natural-rights mode of political philosophy viewed man's nature as primarily passionate or self-interested. It followed that man is an asocial and apolitical animal. By nature, accordingly, man's condition is not one of ordered relations. Since the state is nothing other than an ordering of relationships through establishment of restrictions and jurisdictions, and since it is not natural for man to restrict and order his behavior with respect to others, his natural condition is one of rights. Within a state, law is order and government is the orderer. Neither exists by consent of nature in a natural-rights condition. With human nature viewed as primarily rooted in psychological egoism, self-interest, competition, and conflict are natural. In this mode, the individual exists prior to the community. If the state is to exist it must be created. Rather than being natural, it is an artificial construct of man.

Natural rights proponents therefore are concerned with such

concepts as social contract and popular sovereignty. The source of authority is always from below, from the people themselves. As to claims to authority, they are based on an assertion that there can be no claim to superior significance. Equalitarianism is the rule of this posture.

Man's natural condition is one of rights, which is to say liberty. Whenever rights are considered, the subject of those rights is liberty. For what meaning has liberty but that there are certain areas in which a government may not rightfully act? The latter usage of *right* has a semblance of meaning different from *right* used in the sense of "one's rights." We may say we have a right to this or that, which seems to carry with it not only the notion of correctness, but the additional notion of a claim to something. In fact, "our rights" are actually conceived as rightful possessions. To say a government may or may not rightfully act in a certain sphere, on the other hand, seems only to suggest the notion of correctness (the notion of right or wrong); this is really the opposite side of the coin, for rightness or wrongness is usually determined in relation to transgression upon our rights. Government may not rightfully act because our rights proscribe that action. And these rights become our liberties to the extent that each claim is recognized and permitted by government. Thus the sum total of our liberties, that is, our freedom of action, depends upon spheres of governmental activity.

When individuals have a right to every activity, they are in a condition of license. When they authorize government to restrict certain of those activities, the activities that remain are liberties, or relative degrees of freedom. This freedom also serves as a restriction upon governmental action. It limits that action to specified authorized areas. Thus, as in the natural-law mode, authority is the imputation of permission, and thereby legitimacy, to government action. When government steps outside the area of legitimate action, it commits unauthorized (unrightful) acts.

The American political heritage is one of natural rights. The American Declaration of Independence is the repository of the natural rights statements.

> We hold these truths to be self-evident, that all men are created equal, that they are endowed by their Creator with certain unalienable Rights, that among these are Life, Liberty and the pursuit of Happiness.—That to secure these rights, Governments are instituted among Men, deriving their just powers from the consent of the governed,—That whenever any Form of Government becomes destructive of these ends, it is the Right of the People to alter or to abolish it, and to institute new Government, laying its foundation on such principles and organizing its powers in such form, as to them shall seem most likely to effect their Safety and Happiness.

The thrust of the Declaration is wholly that of the natural-rights posture of political philosophy. All men are created equal and endowed with certain "unalienable" rights. To secure these rights, governments are instituted among men, deriving their just powers from the consent of the governed. Inalienable rights are rights that cannot be given up or taken away. They constitute an area in which individuals have freedom of action and, at the same time, an area that limits government. According to the Declaration, this area comprises the rights to life, liberty and the pursuit of happiness. The right to liberty at first glance seems redundant, that is, the right to rights. Further examination shows that it is not redundant but of the utmost necessity. If there are to be inalienable rights, there must be a right to them. Otherwise they would not be truly inalienable. The Declaration is really saying here that men have a right to the rights of life and the pursuit of happiness. The language of the Declaration makes clear that the foundation of government must be based upon such principles and that governmental power must be organized into such form as will seem most likely to realize "Safety and Happiness" for its people. These are "self-evident" truths, as are the notions that all men are created equal, that governments are instituted among men to secure these rights, and that the people may rightfully overturn a government that does not or cannot procure their safety and happiness.

Locke has long been considered the political theorist who exerted the greatest influence upon our natural-rights heritage. His stature in this respect has been virtually unquestioned. Many go so far as to suggest his influence upon the American Founding Fathers was so great that the United States may be termed a Lockean nation.[1] Yet evidence of this influence is conspicuously missing in the *Federalist Papers*. This is strange, since they constitute the single body of writings by proponents of the Constitution purporting to explain the nature of our government at the time of its founding. It is perhaps all the more strange because there is a strong Lockean tone in other literature of the time.

Of course the expression of such a tone would have been prudent for those harboring hopes of winning political office or popular favor. Locke was, and is, identified with majority rule and liberty, and particularly with the inalienable rights to life, liberty, and the pursuit of happiness. In large part Thomas Jefferson is responsible for that identification. When queried about the origins of notions in the Declaration of Independence, Jefferson responded that they were part of the American mind, and that the Declaration was written for the purpose of expressing them to the world. The authority of that document rested upon sentiments of the day, "whether expressed in conversation, in letters, printed essays, or in the elementary books of public right, as Aristotle, Cicero, Locke, Sidney, or &c."[2]

If we heed Jefferson we must determine who "&c." is. This can be accomplished by looking at what the late Professor Douglass Adair called "The American Statesman's Library." This library primarily resulted from the efforts of James Madison to establish a Library of Congress. Because of restricted funds the library was limited to what Madison, with the advice and concurrence of Jefferson, considered the fundamental political works of that time, works that would provide a substantial background for an American statesman. Many of these books were written by exponents of natural law and of natural rights. Included among them is Hobbes's *Works*.[3] This seems odd since there is little or no mention of Hobbes in relation to the sentiments of the day. Could it have been included only for the purpose of exemplifying the opposing view, the view of a foe of liberty and of the democratic tradition? Or is it possible that Hobbes is included in Jefferson's "&c."?

The latter possibility seems highly improbable, especially when viewed in terms of the results of most scholarship from Hobbes's time to this. Most commentators view Hobbes's norm as power. The standard by which he measured societies, therefore, is held to be their ability to possess and utilize sheer coercive force as a means to attain a simple preservation of life.[4] Moreover, these commentators continue, Hobbes ruled out democracy as the best means of attaining the ends of civil society and preferred monarchy instead. While many[5] accept the Hobbesian view of human nature as that of the Founding Fathers, they insist that any similarity begins and ends there. For them, the American experience can be viewed only as a Lockean solution to a Hobbesian problem.

It will be shown that the traditional views of the extent of Locke's influence are unjustified, particularly when his political thought is compared with that of the Declaration, the Constitution, and the *Federalist Papers*, and that greater similarity to American political heritage exists in the political thought of Hobbes.

There are some who suggest that the Declaration and the Constitution differ greatly in themselves. They view the Constitution as Thermidorean, the product of a conservative reaction to the more democratic principles of the Declaration. The American constitutional experience was not and is not profoundly democratic. After all, the Declaration is a document of revolution while the Constitution founds and thereby stabilizes. Such writings are represented by the works of Samuel Eliot Morison and Henry Steele Commager, and Richard Hofstadter. They are based primarily upon the earlier works of Vernon L. Parrington and Charles A. Beard. Parrington argued that the Founding Fathers not only did not promote democracy, but purposely attempted to avoid it. Beard viewed the results of the Federal Convention as little more than an attempt at protecting the economic interests of those present.[6] It does seem "reasonable" that a document that established government would contain tenets of a less democratic tone than one that overturns a government on a natural-rights basis. Nevertheless, this argument is little more than sophistry. One of the very notions expressed by Jefferson seems to bring Hobbes closer than Locke to the Declaration and, at the same time, seems to suggest that the Constitution must be regarded as at least as democratic as the Declaration. Just prior to his declaration that the United Colonies were and ought to be free and independent, Jefferson wrote: "A Prince, whose character is thus marked by every act which may define a Tyrant, is unfit to be the ruler of a free people." This is to say a *tyrant* is unfit to rule a free people, but it is not to say that a prince is unfit to rule a free people. The natural reading of the Declaration, in fact, is to read it as a criticism of a tyrannical prince and a stated intent to reinstitute just monarchy. This suggests that freedom is compatible with monarchy.

Jefferson argued similarly in a previous part of the Declaration. He stated "that whenever any form of government" became destructive of the ends of civil society "it is the Right of the People to alter or to abolish it, and to institute new Government." It is important to note, as the most prolific writer on *The Federalist*, Professor Martin Diamond did, that Jefferson sees *any* form of government can become destructive of the ends of civil society, that is, destructive of the rights to life, liberty, and the pursuit of happiness. Conversely, any form of government, including monarchy and aristocracy, can attain those ends.

Whenever any form of government becomes harmful to freedom and liberty, thereby failing to attain the ends of civil society, the people have a right to alter or to abolish it. To wholly grasp Jefferson's meaning we must recall that many of his terms carried connotations different from those of the present day. The modern acceptation of "alter" is synonymous with "change." This permits the interpretation of change by means of complete substitution, thereby eliminating all traces of the monarchic form. In the context of the Declaration, however, Jefferson presents what appear to be alternatives, (1) to alter, *or* (2) to abolish. The modern meaning is not quite in harmony with this interpretation. Permitting an equation of the two terms allows the interpretation that the people have the right to alter and abolish. This is to say that the people may alter, thereby abolishing, that form of government. To demonstrate this is not a proper construction, we need look only to the Declaration. Further proof is found in the most prominent dictionary of Jefferson's time: Samuel Johnson's *A Dictionary of the English Language*. "To alter" was listed as: To change; to make otherwise than it is. *To Alter*, seems more properly to imply a change made only in some part of a thing; as to *alter* a writing may be to interpolate it; to *change* it may be to substitute another in its place.

The "altering" of a form of government can mean two things. First, it can mean a modification so that a prince is no longer a tyrant and the ends of civil society are thereby resecured. This modification assumes two types of the monarchic form: tyranny and monarchy. Altering in this sense is changing from a bad form, tyranny, to a good form, monarchy. Second, alteration can be achieved by mixing other forms of government with the present form. Thus the monarchic form would be retained and intermingled with either the democratic or aristocratic form, or both.

According to Samuel Johnson's dictionary, "abolishing" a form of government involves the eradication of that form, as "to annul . . . to put an end to; to destroy." The only alternatives are the substitution of democracy, aristocracy, or a mixed form of both.

Since the stated intent of the Declaration is that the Colonies feel constrained to "*alter* their former Systems of Government" (italics mine), we may infer four possible alternatives: (1) monarchic, (2) monarchic-aristocratic, (3) monarchic-democratic, and (4) monarchic-aristocratic-democratic. One of the possible alternatives is purely monarchic, and none is purely democratic since majority rule hardly can be reconciled with any of those alternatives. We do not find in them that unqualified commitment to democracy that later marked Jefferson's thought. His commitment to freedom is present, but the only explicit mention of it is in connection with monarchy.

Further proof of Jefferson's belief in the compatibility of monarchy and freedom could be seen in an earlier essay, "Summary View of the Rights of British America," written less than two years before. While he saw "the reciprocal advantages" of the connection between Great Britain and America, he argued from the basis of rights derived from nature and not from Rights of Englishmen. In this essay, as in the Declaration, he explicitly associated the idea of a free people with that of a monarchy. There is little reason for arguing that either Jefferson or the sentiments of the day were not attuned to the possibility that men likely would be free under a monarchic form of government. From all of this, there are two important conclusions to be drawn.

First, if it were to be shown that the government established by the Constitution was of mixed form, including a democratic element, then the Constitution would have to be regarded as at least as democratic as the Declaration. Moreover, since in fact that government seeks to nurture the rights to life, liberty, and the pursuit of happiness, and is devoid of monarchic and aristocratic elements, the Constitution must be regarded as the product of a democratic revolution rather than a Thermidorean one.

The second conclusion is that democracy is not synonymous, nor coterminous, with freedom. This understanding is crucial to the primary point of inquiry since Hobbes's thought is considered unlike that of the Declaration because he is a foe of democracy, while Locke's thought appears similar because he is considered a proponent of democracy. If Hobbes can be shown to be a friend of freedom and liberty, albeit a proponent of monarchy, he would move closer to the Declaration. If it could be shown, also, that freedom and liberty are not necessary concomitants of democracy, that some kinds of democracy are in fact repugnant to freedom and liberty, then Locke, even to the extent he remains a champion of democracy, cannot be regarded automatically as a devotee of the same kind of democracy proposed by our Founding Fathers.

We have seen that the persuasion of the Declaration reflects an awareness that all forms of government can be repugnant to freedom and liberty. And it is this awareness that shows the influence of Aristotle's "book of public right." In the *Politics*, Aristotle seemed to argue that there are two kinds of government—good and bad: government directed to the interest of all the people, and government directed to the interest of a particular social class. There are three forms of the first type: kingship, aristocracy, and polity. The three forms of the second type (tyranny, oligarchy, and democracy) are perversions of the forms of the first type. The crucial distinction between good and perverted constitutions turns not upon the kinds of offices held by citizens, nor upon the accidental basis of number, but rather upon whether government is directed to the interest of the whole people or restricted to the interest of a small portion of the people, the ruler or rulers. Accordingly, bad democracy (what Aristotle termed democracy) was directed only to the interest of the many, bad aristocracy (oligarchy) was directed to the interest of the few, and bad monarchy (tyranny) was rule by one in his own interest.[7]

There can be little doubt that Jefferson and the sentiments of the day were attuned to this distinction. Listed first among those acts that define George III as a tyrant is: "He has refused his Assent to Laws, the most wholesome and necessary for the public good." Furthermore, he refused "to pass other Laws for the accommodation of large districts of people." This definition of tyranny, a will independent of society, pursuing its own interest, readily demonstrates Aristotle's influence. By the same token, we see more clearly why the persuasion of the Declaration is that any form of government can either nurture or be destructive of the rights to life, liberty, and the pursuit of happiness.

Locke is considered a champion of democracy because of the belief that he favored a form of majority rule similar to that of the American polity, and, by extension, that this favored form of government was the sort that nurtured rights. We turn now to an examination of Locke's political philosophy in the light of the four truths of the Declaration, that all men are created equal; that they are endowed with certain unalienable rights to life, liberty, and the pursuit of happiness; that governments are instituted among men to secure these rights, with their power derived from the consent of the governed; and that when governments become destructive to these ends, the people have a right to alter or to abolish them.

CHAPTER 2 ☆ LOCKE'S

POLITICAL THEORY REVISITED

THE popularly held belief that Locke's political theory comprises the basis of the American political heritage is difficult to verify when the form of polity he favored is carefully examined. To begin with, Locke is uncertain of the nature of man. For Locke, "men living together according to reason, without a common Superior on Earth, with Authority to judge between them, is *properly the State of Nature.*"[1] Men living together according to reason is men living under the "Law of Nature" (sec. 6). This "Law of Nature" wills "the Peace and *Preservation of all Mankind*" (sec. 7).

The state of nature is seemingly a delightful place. If this is so, why should man want to leave this sort of state? The reason is that some men within this state do not live according to reason, accord, and mutual assistance (sec. 7). These men, whether or not noxious creatures, impose a state of war within the state of nature. Thus men of the reasonable category are given the executive and judicial power of enforcing the law of nature.

Locke gave no argument against those who object to the state of nature and the lodging of such power in the hands of particular men, since men ought not to be (he says it is "unreasonable") "Judges in their own Cases, that Self-love will make Men partial to themselves and their Friends" (sec. 13). He did not at this point explicitly agree that men's "Ill Nature, Passion and Revenge will carry them too far in punishing others" (sec. 13). His answer was: If this is man's nature, we ought not to have absolute monarchy (sec. 13).

Locke did agree explicitly, however, that war and other inconveniencies created in the state of nature because men judge their own cases should be remedied by civil government; yet such a remedy is incompatible with his earlier view of nature and man's nature within it. For Locke to be consistent, some natural mutation must occur that prevents man from living according to reason. This mutation is not, and cannot be, subjective enforcement of the law of nature, for such enforcement is an aspect of living together according to reason.

When men do not live according to reason, they are no longer in a natural state. Locke implies that the inconveniencies are not those of the state of nature, but of an unnatural state, unless Locke is actually saying man was never in a natural state as he defined it: that is, men living according to the dictates of reason.

One might hope to resolve this ambiguity by looking to the solution Locke gave for instability. I fear such hopes are futile. Locke's solution reflects the same uncertainty as his view of human nature. In his own words Locke wrote that the goal of civil society is the mutual preservation of men's "Lives, Liberties and Estates, which I call by the general Name, *Property*" (sec. 123). Men enter civil society because they cannot preserve their "property" in a state of nature because of three deficiencies of that condition. First, the state of nature lacks "an *establish'd*, settled, known *Law*, received and allowed by common consent to be the Standard of Right and Wrong, and the common measure to decide all Controversies" (sec. 124). Second, there is no "*known and indifferent Judge*, with Authority to determine all differences according to the established Law" (sec. 125). Finally, for the most part, the state of nature lacks the "*Power* to back and support the Sentence when right, and to *give* it due *Execution*" (sec. 126).

These insufficiencies are overcome, and civil society created, only "by the consent of every individual" (sec. 96). And "When any number of Men have so *consented to make one Community* or Government, they are thereby presently incorporated, and make *one Body Politick*, wherein the *Majority* have a Right to act and conclude the rest" (sec. 95). Since the majority has the *right* both to determine the standard of right and wrong and to select the common judge and executive, it holds the power to determine the nature of government and civil society, the power to conclude the means of attaining the ends of civil society. Given the additional rights to cut off those parts of the community it finds corrupt (sec. 171), the majority may do whatever it wishes with minorities. Possessing this sort of power, a majority comprised of passionate, vindictive, or self-interested men would give cause for great alarm.

Elucidating the extent of majority activity in a discussion of the three major shortcomings of the state of nature, Locke shows that he did not, in fact, view man as being the reasonable creature one might wish he were. An "established, settled, known, *Law*" is missing from the state of nature, not because none exists, but because man's nature either prevents him from knowing the law, or, where known, from applying it to himself. Locke noted that although the "Law of Nature be plain and intelligible to all rational Creatures; yet Men being biassed by their Interest, as well as ignorant for want of study of it, are not apt to allow of it as a Law binding to them in the application of it to their particular Cases" (sec. 124).

It is also man's nature that gives rise to the need for an indifferent judge. Because men are "partial to themselves, Passion and Revenge is very apt to carry them too far . . . in their own Cases . . . remiss, in other Mens" (sec. 125). Thus Locke came to deny that men in the state of nature live according to reason, as he asserted previously in the treatise.[2]

This seems to explain Locke's reluctance to remain with the position that only the majority may rightfully determine right and wrong. Pitted against the ineluctable will of the majority is the "Prerogative" power that enables the executive "to act according to discretion, for the publick good, without the prescription of the Law, and sometimes even against it" (sec. 160). The executive is also given the power to determine what is right or wrong and what is or is not in the public good—even when the established, settled, known, authorized, common standard of right and wrong prescribes the contrary. Whenever such a conflict raises "a *question* between the Executive Power and the People, *about* a thing claimed as a *Prerogative*; the tendency of the exercise of such *Prerogative* to the good or hurt of the People, will easily decide that Question" (sec. 161). It is a simple matter, therefore, for the people to know when they ought to oppose the executive. Whenever the prerogative is exercised "to make or promote an Interest distinct from that of the publick, [such exercise] gives the People an occasion, to claim their Right, and limit that Power" (sec. 164). In this regard Locke is partially in accord with the right of revolution found in the Declaration. Later he demonstrated complete accord (sec. 149). Locke wrote as if the interest of the public is so obvious that the people not only can determine "easily" what it is, but that they will act only upon what is right as well. If this were true, it should be reflected in the common standard of right and wrong in the first place, the standard the executive, nevertheless, may rightly oppose. Moreover, whether the common standard reflects what is truly right or not is beside the point. It reflects what the people or, more precisely, the majority think is right. The result is inevitable controversy.

Although Locke does not admit this explicitly, implicit proof of his awareness of inevitable controversy is found in his statements about who would resolve that controversy. Addressing himself to the "old Question" of "*who shall be Judge* when this Power is made a right use of?" he wrote a short, but hardly sweet, answer: "there can be no *Judge on Earth*" (sec. 168). And, "as in all other cases where they have no Judge on Earth, [They can only] *appeal to Heaven*."[3] The "appeal to Heaven" held a very precise meaning for Locke, since whenever there is "a Power on Earth, from which relief can be had by *appeal*, there the continuance of the State of War is excluded" (sec. 21). When there is no such appeal, as when appeal can be made only to Heaven, a state of war exists.

So there could be little mistake as to his intended meaning, Locke used the example of Jephtha's appeal as a precise illustration of his point.[4] As Locke's readers knew, this involved conflicting claims to a tract of land that the Israelites had taken by force from the

Ammonites and occupied for some three hundred years. Pointing to the fact that it had been acquired wrongly through conquest, the King of the Ammonites demanded its return or war would result (Judges 11:13). Jephtha responded that he and his contemporaries had not sinned against the Ammonites and, moreover, that possession by the Israelites during the three hundred years made the land rightfully theirs (Judges 11:26–27). Refusing to dispossess Israelites of their property, Jephtha appealed to "the Lord, the Judge, [to] judge this day between the Children of Israel and the Children of Ammon" (Judges 11:27). In the ensuing battle, the Ammonites were adjudged to be wrong.

The appeal to heaven is the unsheathing of the sword, with the side that wins determining the side in the right. On this point, it can be said for Locke that might makes right; but it would be grossly unfair not to admit Locke may have believed right made might. To criticize Locke from within on this point, one must determine whether his theology is an overriding consideration in this treatise. Regardless, it is safe to suggest that the principle of victory in battle determining right is alien to the "American mind," whether in 1776 or at present.

Certainly this can be said: although the majority has the right to determine good or bad in terms of any issue, at any time, the executive has the same right in the exercise of his prerogative, which can be at the expense of the laws. And, in the event of controversy involving the prerogative, civil war is the means of resolution. To the victor belongs the right. This, for Locke, was "well framed government," what he termed "moderated monarchy" (sec. 159). Apparently feeling a need to tone down the implications of his doctrine, Locke was moved to write: "Nor let any one think, this lays a perpetual foundation for Disorder: for this operates not, till the Inconvenience is so great, that the Majority feel it, and are weary of it, and find a necessity to have it amended" (sec. 168). This does not really tell us much. At best we can say coercive power can be employed by the executive until it is conceived by the majority as a "great inconvenience." It is correct to suggest that a majority rule unchecked except by a force of arms by a will independent of society is neither a cornerstone of the American constitutional system, nor a part of the American political heritage. Nor is prerogative—unchecked save through armed rebellion—in the hands of a monarch. Indeed it is only to the extent that alternatives of mixed government may be drawn from the Declaration that Locke's notion of moderated monarchy may be said to be analogous. Thus concerning the matter of governmental form, it is difficult to justify calling Locke a champion of democracy.

In fairness to Locke, certainly, it must be remembered that a democratic tone transcends the matter of form of government. In fact, since many modern-day Americans go so far as to equate libertarianism with democracy, the extent to which Locke championed equalitarianism and a set of inalienable rights to life, liberty, and the pursuit of happiness certainly is of great pertinence to this inquiry. The question at hand, then, is the manner in which Locke squared up to these four notions of "self-evident" truths, to the democratic tone of the Declaration.

The first of the "self-evident" truths is the belief that all men are created equal. Although Locke stated that men are "by Nature, all free, equal and independent,"⁵ he did not view that equality as sufficient to preclude claims to rule based upon the superior abilities of a select few. This is evident in two respects: first, his reasons for rejecting the Aristotelian categories of unmixed forms of government, and, second, the categories to which he turned.

The modern approach to equalitarianism is that, given a view of human nature where the passionate or self-interested proclivities of man are held to dominate his reasonable or altruistic ones, man's passion must be so utilized as to attain the ends of reason. In other words, the pursuit of private interest by each man somehow must be employed to attain the public good. The classicists, on the other hand, held that while most men were dominated by their passionate proclivities, a few were possessed of reason sufficient to dominate their passion. These few were, of course, the *aristoi*. Thus for the classicists, the reason of the *aristoi* had to function to restrain not only their own passions but the passions of the *demos* as well. We already have seen that Locke, like the classicists, believed the passion of the majority could be restrained only by a reasonable external entity via the executor's exercise of his prerogative power. Turning as he did to a will independent of society, to a will insulated from the will of the majority unless overcome by force of arms, Locke turned back to the classical position.

Further indication of Locke's classical posture of inequality is found in his categories of unmixed government: monarchy, oligarchy, and democracy (sec. 132). It is very curious that Locke chose to label government by the few with the appellation, oligarchy, which had meant a perverted form of rule by the *few* in their own interest. But it is startling to find Locke, a supposed proponent of majority rule, admitting a belief in the superiority of an elite few when describing oligarchy as a form in which power is given "into the hands of a few select *Men*, and their Heirs or Successors."[6] As previously noted, unless the claim to equal rights is rooted in a justification of equal abilities, an equality of rights within civil society can be reduced to the sort of equality before the law that allowed Aristotle to favor proportionate equality and distributive justice, and allowed Plato to insist justice consisted in giving his due to every man. In both cases, some men could claim the right to rule resulting from their "equal" treatment as superior or select men.

Locke enlarged upon this position by increasing the number and kind of attributes that make some men superior to others. In section 54 he wrote:

> Though I have said above, Chap. II, *That all Men by Nature are equal*, I cannot be supposed to understand all sorts of *Equality: Age* or *Virtue* may give Men a just Precedency: *Excellency of Parts and Merit* may place others above the Common Level: *Birth* may subject some, and *Alliance* or *Benefits* others, to pay an Observance to those to whom Nature, Gratitude or other Respects may have made it due; and

yet all this consists with the *Equality*, which all Men are in,
in respect of Jurisdiction or Dominion one over another, which
was the *Equality* I there spoke of, as proper to the Business
in hand, being that *equal Right* that every Man hath, *to his
Natural Freedom*, without being subjected to the Will or Authority of any other Man.

It appears that, for Locke, the only equality men possess is an equal
right to natural freedom while in the state of nature. However, once
they come under the authority of a common judge, which is to leave
the natural condition and enter civil society, they lose such equality
or equal right as they ever possessed. To the extent that any equality
can be said to exist within civil society, it is that each man has an
equal right to his due. Since some men have a "just Precedency,"
inequality becomes the rule. While this definition of oligarchy is
similar to Aristotle's view of aristocracy, it differs in at least one
significant respect. The quality making the few superior passes
automatically to their heirs, suggesting an *aristoi* based upon something other than ability.

It is a strong possibility that the claim to superiority is rooted
primarily in property, what Locke termed "estate." Evidence of
this seems present in the text of the *Second Treatise*, which will
be discussed more fully in connection with Locke's understanding
of the "inalienable" rights of man. Further verification can be
found by Locke's association with Sir Anthony Ashley Cooper,
later Earl of Shaftsbury. It is no secret that as Lord Ashley's secre-
tary, Locke helped draft "The Fundamental Constitutions of Caro-
lina." As Samuel Eliot Morison noted, this was the "most fantastic
and reactionary of all colonial frames of government." It provided
for the creation of an oligarchy wherein rank stood in direct relationship to the amount of property one possessed: 300 acres entitled one to be a baron and lord of the manor, 12,000 earned
the title of cassique, and 20,000 hit the jackpot carrying with it the
German title of landgrave. No claim is made here that this association or its results prove Locke an oligarch. What is suggested is

that a consistent theme of oligarchy may be seen in Locke's work at different times.[7]

At any rate, Locke seems to believe there is some thing, or quality, that carried with it the right to rule. Therefore, his conception of equality hardly squares with the Declaration since it does not preclude claims to rule based upon purported superior qualities, whether voiced by a select few or by the executor.

The second of the "self-evident" truths is that all men are endowed by their Creator with certain inalienable rights, among which are the rights to life, liberty, and the pursuit of happiness. This means men are endowed with the rights to safety and happiness, and the right to these rights. In both regards, the differences between Locke and Hobbes are significant. Whereas it is abundantly clear that the right to life is an inalienable one for Hobbes, as shall be seen, it is equally clear that this most basic right of all can be abandoned according to Locke: "*the unjust use of force . . . puts a Man into the state of War* with another, and thereby he, that is guilty of it, makes a forfeiture of his life" (sec. 181).

Moreover, although Locke's rights are alienable, and although they are restricted to life, liberty, and property, these facts do not justify the contemporary position that there is a necessary dichotomy between "early modern doctrines of natural right and the twentieth-century doctrines of human rights."[8] For one, C. B. MacPherson, author of *The Political Theory of Possessive Individualism*, came to this conclusion by elucidating and pointing to the inescapable antipathy between "the earlier triology of natural rights of life, liberty, and property," and the twentieth-century concept of "Human Rights."[9] One need only look to the Public Accommodations Title of the United States Civil Rights Bill of 1963 to see that the rights to life, liberty, and *property* provide little by way of justification for twentieth-century approaches. This bill seeks to reconcile a conflict between competing rights, property rights on the one hand and human rights on the other. The conflict, in other words, is one between the right of property and the right to the pursuit of happiness. It is certain that the Lockean philosophy espousing property rights provides little by way of justifying legislation favoring dispensations contrary to them.

Whereas MacPherson is correct in this respect, his equation of all early modern doctrines of natural rights with only the rights to life, liberty, and property seems questionable, especially when viewed in the light of Hobbes's doctrine of rights. It will be shown that these rights are not only natural, but inalienable, and are not limited to the restrictive category of property. "Human Rights" doctrine could be said to have originated in hedonism properly understood, but there is even less doubt that such doctrine is exposited by Hobbes and well developed in the Declaration. Locke, however, did not dwell on human rights. As MacPherson noted, the doctrine of natural rights of life, liberty, and *property* is rooted in Locke.[10]

In spite of MacPherson's scholarly efforts, it is, perhaps, in this connection more than any other than Locke and Lockism equal Hobbes and Hobbism. The extent to which some have labored to portray Hobbes as a totalitarian who would grant men no more than a sole preservation of life seems matched by the labors of those who have attempted to show that Locke championed government limited by inalienable rights, especially that of happiness.

Even Peter Laslett, editor of the critical edition of *Two Treatises*, has fallen prey to the tendency to read happiness into Locke's thought. Quoting Locke from the *Epistola de Tolerantia*, he translated "*ut mutuo auxilio et junctis viribus harum rerum ad vitam utilium sua cuique privata et secura sit possessio*" as "that by mutual assistance and joint force they may secure unto each other their properties, in the things that contribute to the comfort and happiness of this life." Two terms are of major concern here. The first, *ad vitam*, is one of those omnibus idioms that vaguely can mean "for living," or "for life." At the same time, it must be noted that Renaissance Latin (Erasmian) was devoted to colloquialisms of Plautus, who used *vita* to mean "the supporting of one's self," or "the earning of one's living." The second, *utilium*, means "useful" or "practical," and it is only through forcing its meaning that Laslett finds *faelicitas* in Locke's statement. His rationale appears to be that since *"utilis"* is anything useful, by extension one might say that anything useful brings comfort and happiness. An unforced and more correct translation seems to be: "So that by combining forces to assure mutual support, each man, without harassment, individually can own the practical (or useful) means to pursue his own way of life" (sec. 124).

It is true that Locke was a proponent of natural rights: "Men, being once born, have a right to their Preservation, and consequently to Meat and Drink, and such other things, as Nature affords for their Subsistence" (sec. 25). Not at this point, nor any other, however, does Locke argue explicitly that these are inalienable rights that cannot be forfeited by any word, deed, or act. To the contrary, he explicitly argued that they may be forfeited.[11] This particular statement of rights, moreover, encompasses only a subsistence level, or sole preservation of life.

There is strong evidence supporting a conclusion that Locke held that *every* man had a natural right to no more than a subsistence level of life and that only *some* had a right to more property. The evidence is found in both his previously discussed concept of proportionate equality and in his concept of property. Seemingly not content to hinge justification of unequal possession of property solely upon the elitist claim of proportionate equality, Locke moved to provide further justification from another quarter by rooting it in popular consent. The effect was that both the people as well as "property" itself came to justify possession of more by a select few. Authority exists because the "partage of things, in an inequality of private possessions, man have made practicable out of the bounds of Societie . . . by putting a value on gold and silver and tacitly agreeing in the use of Money."[12] Thus, "Men have agreed to disproportionate and unequal Possession of the Earth . . . [through] tacit and voluntary consent" (sec. 50). Therefore, one's right to possess property, whether at a subsistence level or above and beyond, depends upon the conventional laws of particular states: "For in Governments the Laws regulate the right of property, and the possession of land is determined by positive constitutions" (sec. 50).

Whereas there seems little question that Locke held that some men possessed right to more property than others, there is similarly little doubt that his overriding concern was with *material* properties. In this regard, he went so far as to insist that "the increase of lands and the right of employing of them is the great art of government" (sec. 42). Reading this passage, one is struck by the contrasting view expressed in the Declaration, which portrays the great art as providing for happiness. It is more than mildly interesting that Locke never explicitly suggests that men have a right to the pursuit of happiness. The words happiness and happy appear only four times in the *Second Treatise*, and not in a single instance are they used to represent Locke's own position.[13] Consequently, to determine whether his doctrine of rights is compatible with the right to a pursuit of happiness contained in the Declaration, an examination is necessary to determine whether property can be equated properly with happiness.

There is some difficulty, however, in understanding what he meant by the term *property* because he used it inconsistently. In his chapter on the ends of government, he defined it in the context of the reason men wish to leave the natural condition and enter civil society as their hope "for the mutual *Preservation* of their Lives, Liberties and Estates, which I call by the general Name, *Property*" (sec. 123). Later he added that "By *Property* I must be understood here, as in other places, to mean that Property which Men have in their Persons as well as Goods" (sec. 173). Although he implies it, he is careful not to say that property must carry such meaning in *all* other places. For when the term is examined closely in the various contexts in which it appears, it obviously does not always carry an extended meaning of life, liberty, and property. In point of fact, those times where its meaning is restricted to material possessions outnumber those occasions where it designates its extended trilogistic meaning. There are also cases where it is not clear which meaning it carries.[14]

Even when this difficulty is put aside, however, when all that Locke says about the ends of government and the rights of men is taken together, he addresses no more than life, liberty, and property. The only way one can say that Locke's right to property is tantamount to the Declaration's right to the pursuit of happiness is by insisting that happiness for men is found in material possessions and in the liberty to enjoy them. However, since Locke has insisted that some men have more right to "happiness" than others, and that no one possesses an inalienable right to any of these, life, liberty, or estate (a pursuit of happiness), it is difficult to conclude that Locke's notion of "happiness" for some squares with the Declaration's notion of happiness for all. It seems clear that such a notion of rights, which are both alienable and dependent upon the regulation of conventional laws, hardly squares with the view of rights in the Declaration—even if one supposes that the old trilogy of rights to life, liberty, and property is tantamount to a doctrine of human rights, which necessarily includes the right to a pursuit of happiness.

This examination of Locke and the Declaration regarding their respective views of government, its appropriate ends, and the rights of men suggests the following. Although Locke appears to be a champion of majority rule, he is actually a proponent of mixed government. The Declaration itself, however, is ambiguous with respect to a favored form of government. Its stated intent to alter tyranny could mean an alteration either to mixed government or to the monarchic form. Locke could be said to be compatible with the Declaration in this respect, although his compatibility rests upon inferential evidence.

It is when one inquires into the reasons Locke gave for selecting his favored form of government that he is shown to be not in accord with the Declaration. The reasons turn upon his respective views of human nature, the rights of men, and the appropriate ends of society. In the Declaration, these views are approached on the basis of the four "self-evident" truths.

With respect to the first truth, although Locke originally appears to undercut elitist claims by professing that all men are created equal, a close examination of Locke's concept discloses an impotent doctrine that is nothing other than a basis for proportionate equality. Accordingly, Locke argued explicitly that some men deserve a just precedence because of their superior ability, virtue, or other qualities. While Locke differs from Plato and Aristotle, it is not over the matter of inegalitarianism so much as it is over the question of what sorts of things make some superior to others. This is especially true with respect to property. Where Plato, to the greatest possible degree, would have denied private possessions to the guardians in an apparent attempt to lessen the impact of self-interest upon their behavior (thereby making them better), Locke had no similar reservations. To the contrary, he went so far as to relabel aristocracy as oligarchy and to insist that the very quality making some superior to others is something that can be passed on to their heirs. To the extent that property may be viewed as that distinguishing quality, Locke turned Plato completely about.

Scrutiny of the Lockean doctrine of inalienable rights shows that in three crucial respects Locke is not attuned to the second truth of the Declaration. First, Locke's doctrine is one of *natural* rights, not inalienable rights. Second, following from his inegalitarianism, it is a doctrine that gives more rights to some than to others since by nature some men are superior and naturally deserve more than others. Finally, to the extent that all men share legitimate claims, it is only to a sole preservation, to those things that provide for their subsistence. It is true that a few possess rights to more, but even in this circumstance it is by no means certain that any may claim more than right to life, liberty, and estate rather than right to life, liberty, and the pursuit of happiness. And even the existence of these claims is complicated by Locke's statement that "property" is regulated by conventional law.

With respect to the third truth of the Declaration, although

Locke argued that government is instituted to secure the rights of men, thereby making those rights and the ends of government one and the same, and that governments derive their just powers from the consent of the governed, the ends of government are determined by his doctrine of rights, which is more restrictive than the Declaration. Locke argued that government's great art concerns the increase of lands and the right of employing of them, and he viewed the ends of government as concerning the protection of life, liberty, and estate. Accordingly, he came no closer to the Declaration's stated ends of safety and happiness than security and comfort. Although security is an end for all, comfort is an end only for some. Thus to the extent that enjoyment of material things brings happiness, Locke can be said to say the ends of government are safety for all and happiness for some.

Regarding the last truth of the Declaration, Locke held that the people have a right to revolution whenever government becomes destructive of the ends it was intended to procure. Since Locke's doctrine of the ends of civil society encompasses far less than that of the Declaration, however, the right is similarly restricted both with respect to what may be demanded of government as well as who may demand it. Consequently, most possess the right to resist only when government fails to attain conditions providing a bare subsistence, while a few may resist when government fails to secure their estate beyond that minimal level. Moreover, Locke never seems to have envisioned a need for some of the people to resist the legislature. His view of competing interests within any society is determined by his concept of the one, the few, and the many. He does not seem to conceive of forms of interest other than that of the one, the few, and the public interest. Since the legislation is composed of the people, Locke assumed it would be seeking the interest of both the few and the many. He saw little reason, therefore, for giving some of the people a right to resist the legislative body. Of further interest is the way he blurred the distinction between the few and the many. Ignoring the probability that the few and the many have interests that could be antipathetic, Locke lumped them into a common group, which he referred to variously as the majority, or the people. It is not surprising that so many scholars have suggested that what Locke meant by majority rule was not so much a majority of numbers within civil society, but a majority of weightier or influential individuals comprising a minority of the whole number.

In conclusion, it appears that whether one considers the basic questions in political theory or the presuppositions of human nature in which such questions are rooted, Locke's views are far from squaring up to those of the Declaration. To the extent that he does, it is on unequalitarian and antilibertarian bases. It appears that what has been called Hobbism has been accompanied in the history of ideas by an equally distorted and inaccurate Lockism.

Given ample evidence that there is a Locke and Lockism, it follows that, in spite of extensive commentary upon Locke, especially in recent years, further commentary is clearly warranted. It should prove valuable to begin with an examination of Locke's thought, especially during the years of his association with Lord Ashley. By illuminating the background of the development of Locke's political theory, any oligarchic theme, if extant, could be discovered and explicated. This is similar to Philip Abrams's approach to the theme of "conservatism" in his recent *John Locke: Two Tracts on Government*.[15] The *Tracts*, written in 1660 and suppressed by Locke, seem little other than defenses of nonresponsive government directed toward stifling criticism from below. Abrams, concerned primarily with the freedoms of thought and expression, focused attention upon Locke's later works: *Essays on the Law of Nature, Essay Concerning Human Understanding, An Essay Concerning Toleration, Letters Concerning Toleration* and *The Reasonableness of Christianity*. This study differs from that of Abrams in that it relates a theme of oligarchy to Locke's *Two Treatises of Government*.

There is a strong possibility that much less difference exists between the "Constitutions" and the *Treatises* than previous scholars, including that super sleuth, Peter Laslett, have supposed. This seems a sound conclusion following from apparent oligarchic tenets of the *Second Treatise*. First, even if the question of whether Locke held that men possessed inalienable rights is put aside, the version of rights in the *Second Treatise* concerns government only with the protection of life, liberty, and property, not with life, liberty, and the pursuit of happiness—unless the protection of property is tantamount to happiness. That Locke insisted government is concerned first and foremost with the increase of lands and the right to employ them rather than being primarily concerned with producing conditions favorable to happiness offers further verification of his willingness to limit happiness to mean the enjoyment and protection of material possessions. This would also explain why Locke never used the word *happiness* to elucidate his own position in the *Second Treatise*.

Second, Locke's apparent inequalitarian position not only casts doubt upon the inalienability of men's rights, but certainly results in a form of government which is to a profound degree independent of a majority of society. Whether it be government characterized by a prince's prerogative, as in "moderated monarchy," or government by a select few, as in "oligarchy," it is apparent that some one or some few possess sufficient attributes of superior significance to rightly claim ruling powers.

The theme of property seemingly determines the character of both fundamental tenets: the restrictive sphere of rights and the form of government. Although unquestionably the *Second Treatise* is far less oligarchic than the "Constitutions," it appears more oligarchic than democratic in form and tone. And on this basis it is closer to the "Constitutions" than previously supposed.

Locke did not meaningfully square up to the "democratic" tone of the Declaration, that is, to the four "self-evident" truths. But whereas it is true that Lockism has been misconceived and misinterpreted in the history of ideas, it is also true that the so-called "devilish" and "antilibertarian" Hobbism has been distorted to an even greater extent. Accordingly, a more careful and extensive examination of Hobbes's political philosophy is necessary.

CHAPTER 3 ☆ HOBBES: THE BASIS OF AMERICAN NATURAL RIGHTS HERITAGE

WITH regard to the first "self-evident" truth, equality, Hobbes had argued repeatedly that "Nature hath made men so equall, in the faculties of body, and mind, as that though there bee found one man sometimes manifestly stronger in body, or of quicker mind than another; yet when all is reckoned together, the difference between man, and man, is not so considerable, as that one man can thereupon claim to himselfe any benefit, to which another may not pretend, as well as he." [1] Since man is essentially equal in abilities, he is equal in rights as well. Thus, "all men equally, are by Nature Free." [2]

Hobbes addressed himself here to Plato and Aristotle, insisting that men differ so little in ability that none could claim preferential treatment on the basis of inherent superiority. This obviated, among other things, claims to rule on the basis of superior qualifications of elites such as the *aristoi* or even philosopher-kings.

A great deal of disagreement has arisen over the meaning of the Declaration's phrase, "all men are created equal." Are men created equal in rights, in abilities, or in both? The notion that men can be created equal only in rights seems to offer little in the way of argument against the claims of an *aristoi* or philosopher-king. For even given a natural condition of rights, the wisest, purest, and most able ought to rule, since they best can determine what kind of organization is needed to attain civil society's ends—the rights of all. Hobbes is quite persuasive in arguing that "created equal" means both rights and abilities, since rights are justified by abilities within the context of civil society. Otherwise, equality in rights could be reduced to the sort of equality before the law that allowed Aristotle to favor proportionate equality and distributive justice. At any rate, so far as the first truth is concerned (that all men are created equal), Hobbes's statement is at least as equalitarian as that of the Declaration.

Furthermore, the reasons each man gave for applying specific labels to the various forms of government indicate that in regard to equality, Hobbes was more compatible with the Declaration than was Locke. Locke argued that there were only three unmixed forms of government rather than six as Aristotle purported. So did Hobbes. Locke's basis for doing so differed from Hobbes's, however, since Hobbes insisted there were only three unmixed forms because he thought all men tended to rule in their own interest. Locke's reasoning, on the other hand, was based on the classical theme of innate inequality of men. Hobbes had argued earlier that men were equal in both body and mind and that no man could claim to himself any benefit to which another man could not pretend as well. Equality, then, cannot be measured merely in rights, but in abilities as well. Thus even though both Locke and Hobbes had roughly similar views of the forms of government, their respective rationales are profoundly different.

This is not to say that Hobbes preferred democracy, or that he did not regard monarchy as the best form of government. This he did without question, but not because he viewed monarchy as rule based upon superior ability. The primary reasons he favored monarchy were: (1) because he thought it the form in which rule in the interest of the ruler came closest to rule in the public interest, and (2) because he believed it mitigated the unstabilizing effects of class divisions.[3] This reasoning gave rise to the principle later known as "the invisible hand," which forms one of the primary differences between classical and modern political thought. Not only is this principle missing from the *Second Treatise*, but its very antithesis is present, clearly demonstrating Locke's classical unequalitarian position.

The second "self-evident" truth is that men are endowed with the rights to safety and happiness and with the right to these rights. Although Hobbes is the first theorist systematically to base the proper relationship between individual and government on inalienable rights, it is in this respect, more than any other, that the greatest disparity exists between Hobbes's philosophy and what commentators from his time to the present have said was his philosophy.[4] The extent to which his political philosophy has been said to be totalitarian, absolutistic, atheistic, and other things bad necessitates an extended exposition of his views on inalienable rights. The foundation of those views lies in his notions of the state of nature and the condition of man (which will be dealt with at length in the following chapter). At this point, however, we may say that for Hobbes the state of nature is a state of constant wars. War was not simply the act of fighting, but the period of time in which there existed both a propensity toward and a likelihood of fighting: "the nature of War, consisteth not in actual fighting; but in the known disposition thereto, during all the time there is no assurance to the contrary."[5] The reason for man's unfortunate circumstance in this respect is twofold. While due in part to his nature, man is in a constant state of war primarily because of the natural condition— the result of relations carried on among passionate individuals, each of whom possess complete liberty to use his power as he sees fit. Accordingly, Hobbes insisted that "during the time men live without a common Power to keep them in awe, they are in that condition called Warre."[6] Given man's nature, the effect of one condition (the absence of a common power) necessarily results in a time during which fighting is likely. Since civil society substantially lessens the likelihood of fighting even though man's natural disposition remains intact, the crucial feature of the state of war appears to lie in the likelihood of fighting rather than man's proclivity toward it. This explains why Hobbes believed that whenever men lived in the absence of a common power, they were in a condition of war, and that only the presence of a common power assures the opposite condition, peace.

The state of war, however, is only one of the factors contributing to the wretchedness of the state of nature. Man suffers from more than just the deprivation of an assurance he will not die violently, and he needs more than just the concomitant peace of mind of that assurance. He also suffers from the absence of industry, culture, navigation, commercial intercourse by sea, building, technology, knowledge of geography, account of time, arts and letters. In other words, man's life is solitary, poor, nasty, brutish, and short because he exists without the beneficial fruits of societal institutions. Hobbes often has been misunderstood on this point. By assuming his statement about the nasty and brutish condition refers to the nature of man rather than to the state of nature, some have concluded Hobbes held a very pessimistic view of human nature. This erroneous conclusion will be discussed extensively in the following chapters.

To leave this state of war and to enter civil society, men give up part of their rights possessed in the state of nature and hand them to a common power—the sovereign—in order to have some gain in return. Simply put, they give up the right to each other's life to retain peace and to protect their inalienable rights.

Although Hobbes argued from this contractual basis, he also held that a sovereign who acquired his rule by force possessed as much authority as one who acquired his rule through covenant, thereby placing the subjects of both under equal obligation. This has led most commentators to argue that Hobbes was concerned only with justifying naked force. Illustrative is J. Roland Pennock who wrote that Hobbes argued "speciously in support of the obligation to obey a sovereign who has attained his position by violence [which] prevents him from developing an acceptable theory of political obligation."[7] This interpretation fails to take an underlying and overriding libertarian Hobbesian principle into account. As shall be seen in detail, it is true that Hobbes argued speciously, but his meretriciousness aimed at binding sovereigns as well as subjects. It is interesting to observe that Hobbes has been accepted by neither absolutists nor libertarians, which he appears to have anticipated. Believing that his work was directed to a balance of order and liberty, he felt that proponents of neither faction would find it to their liking: "For in a way beset with those that contend, on one side for too great Liberty, and on the other side for too much Authority, 'tis hard to passe between the points of both un-wounded."[8] To champion liberty in commonwealths created by force, Hobbes argued that men were obliged to obey because in that obedience lay their liberty. By insisting that the rights and consequences of sovereignty are the same in both types of common-wealth, Hobbes not only gave the same rights to each sovereign; he also made the ends of civil society (the consequences of sover-eignty) the same.[9] In other words, *both* sovereign and subject pos-sess the same rights and obligations in either kind of sovereignty. To prove this, Hobbes argued brilliantly, albeit speciously, that even so-called sovereignties by acquisition are established only by consent and choice. This was necessary because he held that the right to sovereignty can never be imposed from above but is de-rived only from the voluntary consent of subjects.

Since in the history of ideas Hobbes has always been portrayed as a staunch defender of absolute monarchy and of sovereigns who attained their rule through force, and since he is considered one of the masters of political thought, why is it that no such sovereign ever employed the Hobbesian justification? The answer is this: Hobbes did not justify sovereignty by acquisition for the purpose of obliging men to a tyrant. To the contrary, it was for the express purpose of obliging a tyrant. On the basis of his justification, those who come to power through force are obliged to protect, promote, and nurture man's inalienable rights to life, liberty, and the pursuit of happiness. A reciprocal obligation of the sovereign is an ineluc-table consequence of the antecedent Hobbesian bases of obligation. For obligation to exist, the acts whereby men divest themselves of the right to total sovereignty must be voluntary. For obliga-tion to be voluntary, men must receive reciprocally some right or other good hoped for in return.[10] Men are obliged to obey the sovereign only when he respects the ends for which the right was transferred or renounced in the first place. Thus on the basis of the Hobbesian formula, sovereignty exists in civil society only when both subject and sovereign are obliged. Indeed, the thing that makes a victor a sovereign is the existence of obligation. When obligation does not exist, all return to the state of nature where there is no common sovereign.

This elucidates a statement by Hobbes which some have interpreted erroneously to mean that, once established, a sovereignty ought never be overturned. Hobbes had addressed himself to *"The Procuration of the Good of the People"* by noting that "The OFFICE of the Soveraign, (be it a Monarch, or an Assembly,) consisteth in the end, for which he was trusted with the Soveraign Power, namely the procuration of *the safety of the people*; to which he is obliged by the Law of Nature, and to render an account thereof to God, the Author of that Law, and to none but him." [11] Considered together with Hobbes's various assertions that the laws of nature oblige in conscience always, but not necessarily *in foro externo*,[12] this statement has led many to infer that if any accounting occurs it is in the next world and not this. The error of such inferences is demonstrated quickly by looking to Hobbes's explicit statements of the relationship between God, nature, natural law, sovereign and subject. In the Introduction to *Leviathan*, Hobbes wrote that nature was "the Art whereby God hath made and governes the World." [13] Immediately before his conclusion to Part II of *Leviathan* he wrote that

> Having . . . spoken of the Naturall Kingdome of God, and his Naturall Lawes, I will adde onely to this Chapter a short declaration of his Naturall Punishments. . . . And hereby it comes to passe, that Intemperance, is naturally punished with Diseases; Rashnesse, with Mischances; Injustice, with the Violence of Enemies; Pride, with Ruine; Cowardise, with Oppression; Negligent government of Princes, with Rebellion;

and Rebellion, with Slaughter. For seeing Punishments are
consequent to the breach of Lawes; Naturall Punishments
must be naturally consequent to the breach of the Lawes of
Nature; and therefore follow them as their naturall, not arbi-
trary effects.[14]

Hobbes here turned Bodin on his head. Rather than viewing an
unjust or negligent Prince as God's instrument for punishing a
wicked people, thereby ruling out a right to rebel, he made the
people God's instrument for punishing a wicked Prince.

Hobbes, with painstaking consistency, wrote of the negligent
government of Princes, not of sovereigns. This is because sovereign
power, by definition, is never unjust, nor can it result in negligent
government. Thus while it is true that a sovereign may never be
required to render an account to subjects of his commonwealth,
this is not to say that Hobbes held that sovereign power cannot
be separated from the man or men who possess it and, once
stripped, that he or they cannot be held accountable by men who
are no longer subjects. In the Preface to *Leviathan*, Hobbes carefully admonished his readers that he would speak "not of the men,
but (in the Abstract) of the Seat of Power."[15] Sovereignty may
never be resisted because by definition it is directed to the procuration of the good of the people. Any power not so directed is not
sovereign power. If there is any major theme in *Leviathan*, it is
that men possess sovereignty only so long as they procure the good
of the people. This is clear in Hobbes's conclusion that "as to the
whole Doctrine, I see not yet, but the Principles of it are true and
proper; and the Ratiocination solid. For I ground the Civill Right
of Soveraigns, and both the Duty and Liberty of Subjects, upon the
known naturall Inclinations of Mankind, and upon the Articles of
the Law of Nature."[16]

Since both sovereignty and the obligation and liberty of subjects
are rooted in human nature and the resultant law of nature, "The
Obligation of Subjects to the Sovereign, is understood to last as
long, and no longer, than the power lasteth, by which he is able

to protect them." [17] Given Hobbes's views that the law of nature requires the protection of the people, that sovereignty exists only so long as the man possessing it can protect the people, that sovereignty exists only so long as the obligation of subjects exists, and that men are naturally inclined to rebel against an unjust or negligent Prince, it is easy to see how the "Civill Right of Soveraigns" is grounded in natural law and man's "naturall Inclinations."

To similarly ground the obligation and liberty of subjects, Hobbes addressed himself "to the particulars of the true Liberty of a Subject; that is to say, what are the things, which though commanded by the Soveraign, he may neverthelesse, without Injustice, refuse to do." [18] His answer is that the obligation of subjects, even to a sovereign, "dependeth not on the Words of our Submission; but on the Intention; which is to be understood by the End thereof. When therefore our refusall to obey, frustrates the End for which the Soveraignty was ordained; then there is no Liberty to refuse: otherwise there is." [19]

This indicates that there are at least two instances in which individuals may rightfully refuse to obey. The first occurs when a sovereign no longer can procure the safety of the people. At this point, all return to a state of nature, a condition in which "sovereign" and "subject" no longer exist. The second instance occurs when, although perhaps capable of procuring the end of civil society, a sovereign demands something antipathetic to that end. Given either of these instances, the notions that Hobbes opposed any right of revolution and supported unqualified obedience seem unwarranted. Not only ought men resist an unjust Prince who has forfeited his sovereignty, they ought to resist even those who retain their sovereignty but in particular instances do not direct themselves to the end of civil society. If any statement of Hobbes's can put to rest the question of whether he believed in a right to revolution, it is found in his assertion that *any* "Civill Law, that shall forbid Rebellion, (and such is all resistance to the essentiall Rights of Soveraignty,) is not (as a Civill Law) any obligation." [20] The obligation not to rebel exists "by virtue only of the Law of

Nature."[21] Since the laws of nature oblige *in foro interno*, the decision to exercise one's right to rebel is always a matter of individual conscience.

In this vein, Hobbes is strikingly close to the third and fourth truths of the Declaration: that governments are instituted to secure the safety and happiness of the people, and that they may be rightfully overturned when they do not or cannot secure them. Moreover, since the ends of civil society, safety and happiness, are approached from the individual perspective as inalienable rights to life, liberty, and the pursuit of happiness as well as safety, there would seem to be complete accord between his principles and the four truths of the Declaration.

In regard to both the inalienability of rights and the notion of happiness, there are significant differences between Hobbes and Locke. Building upon his earlier statements that obligation exists only when men give up right and reciprocally receive some good or right hoped for in return, and that since the transfer or renouncement of right is always a voluntary act, the only object of which is to achieve some good, Hobbes concluded that "Not all Rights are alienable."[22]

> There be some Rights, which no man can be understood by any words, or other signes, to have abandoned, or transferred. As first a man cannot lay down the right of resisting them, that assult him by force, to take away his life; because he cannot be understood to ayme thereby, at any Good to himselfe. The same may be sayd of Wounds, and Chayns, and Imprisonment; . . . And lastly the motive, and end for which this renouncing, and transferring of Right is introduced, is nothing else but the security of a mans person, in his life, and in the means of so preserving life, as not to be weary of it.[23]

The difference between Hobbes and Locke in the second regard is equally striking. In addition to life, Hobbes insisted that there is at least one other inalienable right, the right to a life not wearisome, which logically results from his doctrine of inalienable rights. Since

119239

alienable rights are those that may be given up by the individual
for his own good, it follows that one could not give up a right if
such an action would result in a wearisome life. Although it is
obvious that Hobbes also viewed the right to liberty as inalienable
since no man can give up the right to resist those who would de-
prive him of it by "Chayns" and "Imprisonment," he concentrated
his exposition upon what he viewed as the two basic inalienable
rights: the right to life (man's safety) and the particular kind of
safety following from his precepts. Consequently, most have inferred, in agreement with C. B. MacPherson, that this leaves men
with practically no rights.[24] Such an inference wholly misses what
Hobbes meant by safety: "by Safety here, is not meant a bare
Preservation, but also all other Contentments of life, which every
man by lawfull Industry, without danger, or hurt to the Common-
wealth, shall acquire to himselfe."[25] "Contentments" of life include
not only material things, but mental pleasures as well.[26] With
some degree of truth, one could argue that there is only one inalienable right so far as Hobbes is concerned, safety, as long as "*By
safety is understood all manner of benefits.*"[27] Given the broad
sweep of his concept of safety, however, it makes little sense to
conclude that the individual is left with practically no rights.

Thus far we have examined, in some detail, both Locke's and
Hobbes's views on government, on the end of civil society, and on
the rights of man. Unquestionably, Hobbes is an opponent of democracy and proponent of monarchy. But what concerns us here is
whose views are more attuned to the four truths prescribed by the
Declaration? Since the Declaration does not unequivocally favor
any form of government, Hobbes, because of his reasons for choosing monarchy, is more in accord with the Declaration than Locke.
In regard to the first truth, Locke turned back to the classical position and favored only proportionate equality. His doctrine is therefore more aristocratic, if not oligarchic.

Dissimilarly, Hobbes insisted repeatedly that while there were
differences in the abilities and virtues of men, when all was considered these differences were not sufficient to justify preferential

claims or treatment. Although Hobbes favored monarchy, it was not in consideration of superior ability. Rather, it followed from his belief that no man obtained such superiority. Since all men are equal in ability, and further equally endowed with a proclivity to do that which they believe to be in their own self interest, Hobbes reasoned that the form of government that best took these aspects of man's nature into account, monarchy, was the one most likely to attain the public good. As with Locke, Hobbes did not take recourse to the classical posture of checking the excesses of men through a virtuous entity, whether of the one or the few. In this respect, only Hobbes's concept emerges from a close examination as sufficiently equalitarian to qualify as the classical posture.

With respect to the second truth, whereas Locke's theory is one of inequalitarian natural rights of life, liberty, and property, Hobbes's doctrine is irrefutably one of inalienable rights that extend to all men. To the extent that there is right possessed by some and not others, it is the right to sovereignty. Even this right was originally held by all men, however, and Hobbes argued, albeit speciously, that this natural but alienable right was taken from a man only through his consent. Moreover, continued possession of this right by a ruler depends upon whether all enjoy their rights to life, liberty, and the pursuit of happiness. Besides explicit statements to this effect, his whole political structure is directed to that end.

Hobbes is also in greater accord with the third truth than Locke is. Hobbes viewed the art of government as producing conditions that would attain safety and happiness for all. He explicitly argued that happiness involved more than the enjoyment of material possessions and explicitly insisted that mental pleasures could not be restricted to contemplations about material possessions. Conversely, Locke regarded the ends of government to be only the protection of life, liberty, and estate or, what is the same thing, security and comfort. While security can be shown to be provided for all, comfort is only for some.

Since comfort is to be provided just for the few, the many may resist government only when the latter does not provide a bare subsistence. Furthermore, the right for some of the people to resist the legislative body is not given by Locke, since he assumed that the legislature composed of the people would always seek the interest of both the few and the many. The possibility of antipathetic interests of the few and many was not considered.

Hobbes, on the other hand, foresaw that even a body composed of the people could pursue interests detrimental to the people. Furthermore, he provided a broader base for resisting while rooting the seat of decision as to when even the dictates of a majority are found wanting within each individual. Since the ends of government are the same as the inalienable rights of all men, Hobbes's doctrine is far more individualistic and libertarian than Locke's and closer to the individualism and libertarianism of the Declaration. The right to resist any rule, whether by the one, the few, or the many, or to resist any deputy of any sovereign or sovereign body whenever such rule is not directed to securing society's ends, is a major theme of Hobbes's thought. Regarding the fourth truth, then, Hobbes is again shown to be more attuned than Locke to the Declaration.

We turn now to examine more extensively the presupposition that human nature is rooted in psychological egoism and the consequential impact such a view has upon answers to the basic questions in political theory.

CHAPTER 4 ☆ ON THE

NATURE AND CONDITION OF MAN

H OBBES posited a passionate nature of man. The actions of a man demonstrate not only the objects to which his passions are attached, but the passions as well.[1] Earlier Hobbes insisted "He that is to govern a whole Nation, must read in himself, not this, or that particular man; but Mankind."[2] Hobbes means that the sovereign must see in himself not the *objects* of the passions (for that is his particularity) but rather the *passions*. These are the universal aspects of all men (attributes common to all) and therefore the nature of men, that is, "Mankind."

Over a quarter of a century ago, Leo Strauss discussed the significance of Hobbes's awareness of such a passionate nature. It was "the first peculiarly modern attempt to give a coherent and exhaustive answer to the question of man's right life."[3] Strauss later retracted this view, feeling Machiavelli deserved this laurel, not Hobbes.[4] Following Machiavelli, Strauss argues that man's nature has changed to become anything but reasonable, and this change is due to man's condition, which also has changed. As Professor Strauss asserts, if man in his natural condition is reasonable, the community is logically prior to the individual. This is to say, man is reasonable, a political-social animal, and therefore in a natural condition of restriction. Man's condition is not license, but limitation stemming from law, that is, natural law.

Strauss's suggestion that Machiavelli's notion of a changed condition, which alters man's nature and places him in a situation of natural rights, ignores the changed condition. Man has become a passionate animal. But that animal, no longer in the previous natural condition, is now in a condition of civil society. This is to say that man has become apolitical due to his political condition, which is one of restriction, not one of right. This implies two things. First, although man is passionate, he is in a condition of restriction due either to his natural condition of prior reasonableness and restriction, or to the present condition of civil society, which is also a condition of restriction. Second, it follows that neither interpretation provides a basis for an assertion of natural rights. Man is in neither case by nature apolitical.

Since Strauss first saw the total implications in Hobbes he now attributes to Machiavelli, it could be that he read Machiavelli through Hobbes-colored glasses. The implications of a passionate nature and the awareness of an essential quality of man were the creatures of Hobbes, not Machiavelli. If Machiavelli is credited as the first to conceive man's nature as passionate, thereby placing man in a condition of natural right, where is this notion present in Machiavelli's political system? Where are the limits upon governmental action that are the necessary concomitants of individualism or libertarianism?

Strauss also argues that everyone is by nature concerned with his own well-being.[5] Although men ought to see that society is most conducive to this well-being, they need additional selfish incentives to make them comply.[6] What is needed are institutions rewarding activity conducive to the common good and punishing activity contrary to it.[7] The common good is not concern for the individual or a libertarian sphere. It is concern for "the well-being of the large majority of the people and of the great."[8] Strauss does not seem greatly concerned about why the well-being of the large majority of the people is compatible with that of the great. This compatibility seems unlikely since well-being is a man's concern "with his preservation, his security, his ease, his reputation, his honor, his glory."[9] If a man can further any aspect of his well-being at the expense of the well-being of others, he likely would do it. The only restriction upon this perverse activity is punishment. Fear (reason), not Machiavelli's combination of fear and love (passion), then, be-

comes the only incentive that makes man sacrifice his selfish interest
to the common good.

A related question is the problem of men in government. Why
could or will men in government ever bother to direct themselves
to the common good? Such action seems unlikely, since everyone is
"by nature concerned only with his own well-being." [10] The answer
is that governors ought to be "men of great virtue, i.e., of greatness
and nobility of mind, and therefore revered as good at protecting
the good and the friends, and at harming the bad and the enemies.
The task of the political art consists in providing not only that the
most able men can rise to the highest but above all that they be
kept good while they occupy such positions." [11] At first glance,
keeping the rulers "good" appears little more than a noble sentiment in light of the selfish nature of man. It *is* something more,
but not much. For virtue, or goodness, is "the ability to acquire
for oneself the highest glory and hence to acquire for one's state
whatever makes it strong, prosperous, and respected." [12] This is
certainly consistent with a passionate nature of man. But there are
other objects of man's passion: preservation, security, ease, pleasures, reputation, and honor. Keeping a ruler virtuous is really preventing him from placing greater value on other pleasures, such as
personal wealth and riches. Thus portrayed, however, man is still
seen by nature to be in a state of natural law or restriction. The
shadow of the classical tenets of political philosophy is still dis-
cerned.

It is only with the "modern" period that the break with previous
theory is complete. The tenets of this period are: (1) man is by
nature passionate, (2) so man is apolitical, (3) therefore the individual is logically prior to the community, and (4) thus man is in
a natural state of rights. And these should properly be attributed
to Hobbes.

There is another equally important prerequisite of modern libertarian thought, equalitarianism. The simple fact of a passionate
nature does not pave the way for libertarian individualistic thought;

if there are within a given society men who are vastly superior to their fellow in virtue, excellence, or physical and mental abilities, it follows that those who are excellent should have preferential claims to various benefits within society, at least a claim to determine public policy. How can one argue for limited government, or for placing individuals above government, when that government is made up of superiors who are ruling inferiors? But modern political philosophy is certainly one of individualism. Moreover, insofar as individualism and libertarianism depend upon natural rights doctrine and equalitarianism, and insofar as democratic thought depends in turn upon individualism and libertarianism, democratic thought is based upon a notion of essential equality. Men are not only created equal, they are equal.

So far we have seen that Hobbes viewed man's nature as passionate. It remains for us to trace this notion and view its implications to determine whether he has little relation to the American political heritage.

Hobbes began his chapter on the natural condition of man by noting that though some were manifestly stronger in body or quicker in mind than others, yet "when all is reckoned together, the difference between man, and man, is not so considerable, as that one man can thereupon claim to himselfe any benefit, to which another may not pretend, as well as he." [13] The equality of men is the basis of equal claims to things. We have often heard someone exclaim, "Why should you get it? I am as good as you." It is only when men are no better than others that we are equally qualified to rule, or to make claims to things.

Hobbes believed an essential equality among men gave rise to an equality of hope in attaining ends, the principal one being man's own conservation. Nevertheless, men outside civil society who desired the same thing or end became enemies and attempted to destroy or subdue one another. Thus in man's natural state, equality bred diffidence. The only course of action left to a man in the face of this diffidence was an aggrandizement of his power to the point where he could see no other power great enough to endanger him. [14]

This partially explains why Hobbes believed there existed "a generall inclination of all mankind, a perpetuall and restlesse desire of power after power, that ceaseth onely in Death." [15] Competition for objects common to men's desires leads to competition for acquisition of the means of attaining those objects, and the means are just this: power. "The Power *of a Man*, (to take it Universally,) is his present means, to obtain some future apparent Good." [16] To Hobbes, the complete subjectivist, the Good was defined by each particular man as he saw it. The fact that it may or may not have resulted in a benefit for him is utterly beside the point.

Another aspect of the explanation of man's inclination to acquire power also relates to competition and diffidence. For once a man has acquired the object of his desire, he wants "not to enjoy once only, and for one instant of time; but to assure forever, the way of his future desire." [17] Once he has it, he wishes to ensure the means of keeping it. "Desire of Power after power" exists not because man cannot be "content with a moderate power: but because he cannot assure the power and means to live well, which he hath present, without the acquisition of more." [18] Hobbes paralleled this statement in chapter 13. There are "some, that taking pleasure in contemplating their own power in the acts of conquest, which they pursue farther than their security requires; if others, that otherwise would be glad to be at ease within modest bounds, should not by invasion increase their power, they would not be able, long time, by standing only on their defence, to subsist." [19]

It is only some men, not all, who derive pleasure from an inordinate amount of power. Only some have an insatiable desire for power. The actions of these men cause others to pursue power after power above and beyond a moderate amount. In an earlier chapter on the passions of men, Hobbes defined "Glory" as the mental pleasure, "Joy, arising from imagination of a mans own power and ability." [20]

Power, when related to glory, is no longer a means to an end. It is an end in itself. Insofar as it is a means, it is a means of acquiring more of itself. The power-glory relationship serves to elucidate

Hobbes's earlier admonishment not to confuse individual striving after particular objects with a universal aspect of man. For most men, power represents the means of attaining the objects of their desires. For some, it is the object of their desire.

Examining the nature of man, and of some men, Hobbes found three principal causes of quarrel: competition, diffidence, and glory.[21] "The first, maketh men invade for Gain; the second, for Safety; and the third, for Reputation. [Hobbes had earlier defined Reputation as an instrumental power, an acquired form of power or means of obtaining some future good.][22] The first use Violence, to make themselves Masters of other mens persons, wives, children, and cattell; the second, to defend them; the third, for trifles, as a word, a smile, a different opinion, and any other signe of under-value, either direct in their Persons, or by reflexion in their Kindred, their Friends, their Nation, their Profession, or their Name."[23]

The most interesting, and perhaps most unnoticed, notion here is that the desire of "power after power" beyond a "moderate" amount in all men is due not to their nature, but to a social condition of human relations. "The life of man, [is not] solitary, poore, nasty, brutish, and short"[24] because man's nature is nasty and brutish. Rather, it is due to the social condition in which man finds himself, a relationship of men with other men. Some men have objects of their passions that cause them to pursue aggrandizement of power *ad infinitum*. Others come into a similar pursuit, not because of their nature, but because of their relationships with men of the "glory" category. Power is sought as a means of defense, and is still viewed by these men as a means.

The primary cause of man's "poore" condition is the social condition. As noted earlier, during the time men live in this condition, which is a situation of relations among men in the absence of a common coercive power,[25] "they are in that condition which is called Warre; and such a warre, as is of every man, against every man."[26] Where there is no civil society, there will be found a condition of war.[27] "In such condition, there is no place for Industry;

because the fruit thereof is uncertain: and consequently no Culture of the Earth; no Navigation, nor use of the commodities that may be imported by Sea: no commodious Building; no Instruments of moving, and removing such things as require much force; no Knowledge of the face of the Earth; no account of Time; no Arts; no Letters; no Society; and which is worst of all, continuall feare, and danger of violent death." [28] It is not man's nature but his condition that prevents the realization of these things necessary for "commodious living." Only in this light can we understand two following statements, which appear disharmonious.

Hobbes first suggested "Nature" disassociates and renders "men apt to invade, and destroy one another." Then he insisted that he was not accusing "man's nature in it." Nature in the first statement refers to a natural condition (the absence of a common coercive power) in which man's passionate nature can only lead to a condition of war. Life is poor because in a condition of war man has little time to develop industry, or the institutions that help him acquire those things necessary to commodious living. Because of this and the continual fear and danger of violent death, man's life is solitary, poor, nasty, brutish, and short. The original cause is a condition—men living together in a situation of relations characterized by the absence of a common coercive power. The immediate cause is man's passionate nature, which in this sort of condition gives rise to competition, diffidence, and glory. And these, in turn, are the direct causes of war.

We must also pause to take stock of the shortcomings of the "ill condition, which man by meer Nature is actually placed in." [29] First and foremost is the danger of violent death and its concomitant fear. Thus it could be argued that the purpose of civil society for Hobbes is only preservation of life, had he said no more. Hobbes, however, said a great deal more. This ill condition also lacks industry, culture, navigation, arts, and letters. It lacks those things or institutions necessary to attain what Hobbes described as "all contentments of life." If, as Hobbes claims, the intent of civil society, or the Leviathan, is to overcome these shortcomings, to eradicate this ill condition, Hobbes obviously is addressing himself to something far beyond a simple preservation of life.

Later, Locke unfairly criticized (if in fact his remarks were addressed to Hobbes and not Filmer) Hobbes's "a state of nature," insisting upon a distinction between a state of nature and a state of war. As we can see, Hobbes also was aware of this distinction. Hobbes is saying that any condition wherein men have relationships in the absence of a common coercive power and with complete and utter liberty (the only proper understanding of Hobbes's "state of nature") will be characterized by a condition of war. The state of nature is a state of almost complete right, almost a state of license. There is one right which man does not possess, the right to knowingly take his own life. Such a condition of right, or almost complete lack of restriction, is obviously one wherein there is a continual tendency for men to fight with their neighbors. But the condition, properly understood, is one of complete right to deal with one's neighbors in any manner he chooses. This leads to a concomitant condition of war, as defined by Hobbes. It will be shown later that there is little or no difference between Hobbes and Locke on this view.[30] Hobbes and Locke, however, can be seen to disagree sharply on the essence of the state of nature. For Hobbes this condition will always be characterized by an attendant condition of war. As we shall see, Locke is "confused," not only about the state of nature, but the state of war as well.

Once Hobbes posited a passionate nature of man leading to a condition of war, what possibility did he see that could cause or allow men to enter into a covenant, thereby escaping the state of nature? In other words, how can a "passionate man" or why does a "passionate man" follow a course of action normally ascribable only to a "reasonable man?" This may be viewed as a fundamental inconsistency in Hobbes. To take this position, however, indicates not only a misunderstanding of what Hobbes meant by the passionate nature of man, but a misunderstanding of what most men meant by a passionate nature.

To explain the latter notion, Plato's view of man's "reasonable" nature may be helpful. Man is a reasonable animal, but this does not mean wholly reasonable. Man also has a passionate aspect. Reason functions to restrain the passions, which is not to say passion will never assert itself to cause or control action, nor that passion is not a part of man. By the same token, a passionate nature of man does not deny a coexisting reasonable aspect. This is precisely the view that accurately represents Hobbes. For Hobbes summed up his statements about the state of nature by saying: "Thus much for the ill condition, which man by meer Nature is actually placed in; though with a possibility to come out of it, consisting partly in the Passions, partly in his Reason."[31]

The passions inclining men to peace are both aversion and appetite. The precise sort of aversion is fear—the fear of death. The appetite is a desire for those things necessary to commodious living; and a hope through industry to attain them.[32] Reason's function consists of suggesting "convenient Articles of Peace, upon which men may be drawn to agreement."[33] To Hobbes these articles were the Laws of Nature, that is, "dictates of Reason, men use to call by the name of Lawes; but improperly: for they are but Conclusions, or Theoremes concerning what conduceth to the conservation and defence of themselves; whereas Law, properly is the word of him, that by right hath command over others."[34]

The discussion of "Mentall Discourse" shows the distinction between reason and passion; "Mentall Discourse" is the "*Consequence*, or Trayne of Thoughts . . . that succession of one Thought to another."[35] It is the thought process whereof there are two types.[36]

The first type is unguided. It lacks direction or purpose and meanders from one thought to another.[37] The example Hobbes used to illustrate this sort of thought involved both mental and verbal discourse. Recalling a conversation in which the current civil war was the topic, he noted that one of the discussants suddenly asked the value of a Roman penny. At first this question might have seemed impertinent or irrelevant to the conversation. But its coherence could be seen by tracing the dependence of one thought upon another. "For the Thought of the warre, introduced the Thought of the delivering up the King to his Enemies; The Thought of that, brought in the Thought of the delivering up of Christ; and that again the Thought of the 30 pense, which was the price of that treason; and thence easily followed that malicious question."[38] The first type of thought is unguided because there is no passionate thought to govern or direct those thoughts following it.

The second type is regulated, or guided, thought process. It has design and direction.[39] The things we desire or fear make a strong impression on our thoughts. Using desire as an illustration Hobbes writes: "From Desire, ariseth the Thought of some means we have seen produce the like of that which we ayme at; and from the thought of that, the thought of means to that mean; and so continually, till we come to some beginning within our own power. And because the End, by the greatnesse of the impression, comes often to mind, in case our thoughts begin to wander, they are quickly again reduced into the way: . . . that is to say, in all your actions, look often upon what you would have, as the thing that directs all your thoughts in the way to attain it."[40]

Passion plays a crucial role in thinking. It provides purpose and thereby direction to thought. Reason can best be understood, and more clearly distinguished from passion, when seen in relation with "Remembrance," "Prudence," and "Signes." Passionate thought is a seeking "of the causes, of some effect, present or past; or of the effects, of some present or past cause."[41] "Remembrance" is passionate thought attuned to the past. "Prudence" is the application of "Remembrance" to the future. By way of elucidation, Hobbes observed that "Sometime a man desires to know the event of an action; and then he thinketh of some like action past, and the events thereof one after another; supposing like events will follow like actions. As he that foresees what will become of a Criminal, recons what he has seen follow on the like Crime before; having this order of thoughts, The Crime, the Officer, the Prison, the Judge, and the Gallowes."[42] Given a present antecedent, in this case a criminal, "Prudence" consists of the application of memory of a past similar antecedent with its attendant consequences, prison, gallows, et cetera, to produce a prediction of what will likely occur to the criminal of the present. This is the seeking of consequences of the future.[43] Thus, "Prudence is a *Praesumtion* of the *Future*, contracted from the *Experience* of the time *Past*."[44] The most prudent men are the most versed and studied in matters of antecedents and consequences. Which is to say the most prudent men are those with the most "Signes" to predict with.[45]

"Signes" are either the antecedent event or the consequence of that antecedent. They are the bricks used to build predictions of future events stemming from present causes, or predictions of causes needed to produce a future event based upon causes and events of times past.[46]

At this point we might well question the need for reason at all. For it seems possible man can leave the condition of nature solely on the basis of passionate thought. The desire of commodious living, the hope of attaining it, and the fear of death certainly give the necessary push-pull causing man to want to leave. "Prudence" and "Remembrance" enable man to see the necessity of something else, but here is the rub. What something else? Passionate thought is based upon experience of the past. Men living in the natural condition can look to past experience for evidence of the need of something new. However, they cannot say just what that something new is. There is no past experience of civil society. The role of reason is to determine what that something new is. Passion can tell men it is the opposite of war—peace, but it cannot tell men what "Articles of Peace" serve to construct a condition of peace, that is, a condition of civil society. "When a man *Reasoneth*, he does nothing else but conceive a summe totall, from *Addition* of parcels; or conceive a Remainder, from *Substraction* of one summe from another: which (if it be done by Words,) [symbols][47] is conceiving of the consequence of the names of all the parts, to the name of the whole; or from the names of the whole and one part, to the name of the other part."[48]

Reason begins with parts, the individual and what he represents, and proceeds through their consequences to the whole—civil society. This reason is not right reason. It is the subjective reasoning of a particular man based upon nothing but "educated guesses."[49] But only through reason can man enter civil society. "The Light of humane minds is Perspicuous Words . . . *Reason* is the *pace*; Encrease of *Science*, the *way*; and the Benefit of man-kind, the *end*."[50] Through reason man approaches science, which is "a knowledge of all the Consequences of names appertaining to the subject in hand,"[51] in this case, man. Thereby we understand Hobbes's statement that the science of the laws of nature "is the true and onely Moral Philosophy."[52]

Hobbes says two things about "natural law." First, it is the result of *his* own reasoning. Second, it begins with the individual and proceeds to an understanding of civil society. It is this second notion that is correctly termed the most revolutionary theory of the age. Although it is logically possible to begin with the individual and arrive at a need for "absolute" power, this is not what Hobbes does. And because of this, his individualism is the most revolutionary theory of the age.

The revolution began with a restatement of the natural condition of man, a condition of war, of everyone against everyone.[53] Man is in a condition of complete liberty. This is to say each man has the liberty to use his power, as he wishes, for the preservation of his life.[54] Consequently, each governs himself "and there is nothing he can make use of, that may not be a help unto him, in preserving his life against his enemyes."[55] This is the "RIGHT OF NATURE," commonly called *Jus Naturale*.[56] It follows that "every man has a Right to every thing; even to one anothers body. And therefore, as long as this naturall Right of every man to every thing endureth, there can be no security to any man."[57] The logical consequence of an antecedent passionate nature of man is a natural condition of rights for Hobbes, whereas for Plato and Aristotle, the logical consequence of a reasonable nature of man was a natural condition of law. For as Hobbes knew, right is liberty, and liberty is the absence of impediments to doing as one wishes. Law is restriction, one of those things that impedes man from doing things. "They that speak of this subject [confound] *Jus*, and *Lex*, *Right* and *Law*; yet they ought to be distinguished; because RIGHT, consisteth in liberty to do, or to forebeare; Whereas LAW, determineth, and bindeth to one of them: so that Law, and Right, differ as much, as Obligation, and Liberty."[58] To move from this sort of natural condition to a "law of nature" is to move from right to law, from liberty to restriction. But the restriction must be the logical consequence of the individual's liberty. Thus a law of nature is a rule arrived at through reason "by which a man is forbidden to do, that, which is destructive of his life, or taketh away the means of preserving the same."[59] It also contains restrictions on further subjective determination of what each most needs to preserve himself.[60] The consequence is the "generall rule of Reason," "*That every man, ought to endeavour Peace, as farre as he has hope of obtaining it; and when he cannot obtain it, that he may seek, and use, all helps, and advantages of Warre.*"[61]

There are two "branches" of this rule. The first is the fundamental law of nature—"*to seek Peace, and follow it.*"[62] The second is the "summe" (the whole) of the right of nature—to use "*all means we can, to defend our selves.*"[63] The consequence of the fundamental law of nature is the second law, which is the basis of social contract. The first law commands all men to endeavor to achieve peace. The second law commands "*That a man be willing, when others are so too, as farre-forth, as for Peace, and defence of himselfe he shall think it necessary, to lay down this right to all things; and be contented with so much liberty against other men, as he would allow other men against himselfe.*"[64] Hobbes reasoned that as long as men had the right to do anything they wished, they would remain in a condition of war. If some would not relinquish the right to all things, there was no reason for others to do so. "For that were to expose himselfe to Prey, (which no man is bound to) rather than to dispose himselfe to Peace."[65] Hobbes illustrated the second law with, for us, an inverted version of the golden rule. What you wish others to do to you, do to them.[66]

When a man lays down his right, he does nothing more than divest himself of the liberty to prevent someone else from acquiring the benefits of the same right.[67] For in giving up his own right to *any* means of acquiring those things, he is merely giving others what they already had by nature.[68] "So that the effect which redoundeth to one man, by another mans defect of Right, is but so much diminution of impediments to the use of his own Right originall."[69]

There are two ways of laying down right: by renouncing it; or by transferring it. Right is renounced when the individual does not care who will benefit therefrom. Right is transferred when the individual intends the benefit resulting from that transfer to go to a certain person. In either case, the individual is "OBLIGED, or BOUND, not to hinder those, to whom such Right is granted, or abandoned, from the benefit of it: and that he *Ought*, and it is his DUTY, not to make voyd that voluntary act of his own."[70] Hobbes demonstrated here his awareness of the nature of obligation and of authority. In his little book on political obligation,[71] Joseph Tussman argued for what he termed a theory of political obligation as distinguished from a theory of political behavior. For Tussman, the former theory necessitates the political education of both citizens and government agents. The model most congenial to such a theory is that of the voluntary organization, thereby ruling out models based upon norms of power or custom. A theory of obligation attempts to delineate the demands of the political role and propriety in response to those demands, obligations, and duties. Thus obligation, as authority, carried with it the notion of ought. If there is to be an ought, and this is what authority is based upon, there must be a choice. For in any situation in which authority enters, man has an option. The sense of oughtness and option in a man is dependent upon his values.

To Hobbes, ths shared notion of what ought to be is peace and commodious living. These are the most significant values in man. To attain this condition man voluntarily transfers his right. Accordingly, Hobbes demonstrated a voluntary transfer in sovereignties by acquisition as well as in sovereignties by institution. This is why Hobbes can say man "Ought" not hinder those to whom the right was transferred. Obligation exists when men transfer right and receive reciprocally some right or other anticipated good in return.[72] Since the transfer of right is a voluntary act, the only object of the transfer is some good. Therefore not all Rights are alienable;[73] man has at least the inalienable right to life. But Hobbes also insisted there is at least one other paramount right of man: a preservation of life that is not wearisome.

At first this seems unclear, since it is introduced as part of the motive for the transfer of right. But this confusion is resolved by observing that the right to a life not wearisome is a second aspect of "the security of mans person." Furthermore, those rights that are alienable are those that can be given up by an individual aiming to promote his own good. An individual could hardly aim at his own good and give up a right that protects him from a wearisome life. Recalling that the Right of Nature includes the notion of subjective determination of the aptest means of realizing self preservation, the right to avoid a wearisome life is more obviously an inalienable right. What is given up is the subjective determination of the aptest means (of which part is a life not wearisome), and not the means. Further proof is found in what happens when a man lays down his right. He divests himself of the liberty of preventing others from acquiring benefits stemming from that right. There are two inalienable rights. The first is life, that is man's safety. The second is the particular sort of safety Hobbes deduced from the first. "By Safety here, is not meant a bare Preservation, but also all other Contentments of life, which every man by lawfull Industry, without danger, or hurt to the Commonwealth, shall acquire to himselfe."[74] "Contentments" are more than simply material things; they also consist of mental pleasures and are listed in the discussion of the shortcomings of the condition of mere nature. The only term accurately representing these contentments of life is happiness. Hobbes was more explicit in *De Cive* than in *Leviathan*. Under the title, "That by safety is understood all manner of benefits," he said that "by *safety* must be understood, not the sole preservation of life in what condition soever, but in order to its happiness. For to this end did men freely assemble themselves, and *institute* a government, that they might, as much as their human condition would afford, live delightfully."[75] The benefits of which Hobbes spoke fell into four kinds:

> That they be defended against foreign enemies. That peace be preserved at home. That they be enriched as much as may consist with public security. That they enjoy a harmless liberty. For supreme commanders can confer no more to their civil happiness, than that being preserved from foreign and civil wars, they may quietly enjoy that wealth which they have purchased by their own industry.[76]

At this point we can see Hobbes's teaching most certainly is consonant with the notions of the Declaration of Independence. Hobbes began by asserting that man found himself in a natural condition of right, due to his passionate nature. He entered civil society "by Covenant only, which is Artificiall."[77] He voluntarily contracted some of his rights away, but even in civil society there are two he retained. He has a right both by nature and by contract to life and happiness. I said previously that liberty was best understood as the right to rights, and the sum total of those rights. Thus the end of the *Leviathan* is to create a condition in which man's activities are characterized by the rights of life, liberty, and the pursuit of happiness. Furthermore, the original contract serves two purposes: (1) it limits government from exercising total power, and (2) it establishes government by consent. There can be little doubt this government has authority.

But there remains one troublesome thing. Man pursues happiness by lawful industry. He or they who make the law determine what is lawful and what is not. Through this means, man's pursuit could be limited to only a bare preservation in spite of the covenant. Hobbes could say the laws of civil society ought to reflect the law of nature, but what caused him to believe this would actually occur? This is especially doubtful when viewed in terms of Hobbes's concept of "unlimited sovereignty." Moreover, there is the problem of the manner in which sovereignty is acquired, whether by consent or by force.

A system based upon unlimited sovereignty, derived by force, does not seem consistent with libertarian theory unless an underlying principle can be found which overcomes its antilibertarian aspects. Concerning the notions of sovereignty by consent or force, Hobbes remarked: "The attaining to this Soveraigne Power, is by two wayes. One, by Naturall force; as when a man maketh his children, to submit themselves, and their children to his government, as being able to destroy them if they refuse; or by Warre subdueth his enemies to his will, giving them their lives on that condition. The other, is when men agree amongst themselves, to submit to some Man, or Assembly of men, voluntarily, on confidence to be protected by him against all others. This later, may be called a Politicall Common-wealth, or Common-wealth by *Institution*; and the former, a Common-wealth by *Acquisition*." [78]

This raises a question about Hobbes's previous definition of "Common-wealth," which appears irreconcilable with the possibility of common-wealth created through force rather than consent. His definition arose from an objection to Aristotle's thesis that ants, bees, and men are political creatures by nature. He granted that ants and bees are by nature political. [79] But with man, a continual competition for "Honour and Dignity" prevents men from having political associations in the absence of a common power. Thus "the agreement of these creatures is Naturall; that of men, is by Covenant only, which is Artificiall: and therefore it is no wonder if there be somewhat else required (besides Covenant) to make their Agreement constant and lasting; which is a Common Power, to keep them in awe, and to direct their actions to the Common Benefit." [80]

The agreement of men is *artificial*. Civil society is not the way of man's nature. Therefore, civil society is "created," and created only through "Covenant." Men

> conferre all their power and strength upon one Man, or upon
> one Assembly of men, that may reduce all their Wills, by
> plurality of voices, unto one Will: which is as much as to say,
> to appoint one Man, or Assembly of men, to beare their Per-
> son; and every one to owne, and acknowledge himselfe to be
> Author of whatsoever he that so beareth their Person, shall
> Act, or cause to be Acted, in those things which concerne the
> Common Peace and Safetie; and therein to submit their Wills,
> every one to his Will, and their Judgements, to his Judgement.
> This is more than Consent, or Concord; it is a reall Unitie
> of them all, in one and the same Person, made by Covenant
> of every man with every man, in such manner, as if every man
> should say to every man, *I Authorise and give up my Right
> of Governing my selfe, to this Man, or to this Assembly of
> men, on this condition, that thou give up thy Right to him,
> and Authorise all his Actions in like manner.*[81]

When this is accomplished, "the Multitude so united in one person, is called a COMMON-WEALTH."[82] This "one person,"
whether a man or an assembly of men, is the "Soveraigne." Within the "Soveraigne" is the essence of the commonwealth, which
is defined as "*One Person, of whose Acts a great Multitude, by
mutuall Covenants one with another, have made themselves every
one the Author, to the end he may use the strength and means of
them all, as he shall think expedient, for their Peace and Common
Defence.*"[83] We see here an important and consistent theme: the
sovereign power must be used for the safety of all.

But if a commonwealth can be created only through consent,
and by means of a covenant, how can Hobbes suggest that there is
such a thing as "Common-wealth by acquisition?" Furthermore,
how can the acts of the sovereign be viewed as authorized? The

unity of will occurs through the acknowledgment of each subject, through mutual agreement and consent.

It is, for the most part, this apparent inconsistency on the notion of sovereignty by acquisition that has been the primary cause of Hobbes's antilibertarian label. For this appears to be none other than the establishment of "legitimate" government through naked force. Such government renders meaningless any notions of authority or obligation in Hobbes's system since they attach to government only through voluntary acquiescence.

I believe the answer lies in the very statement that to us seems so inconsistent. A commonwealth by acquisition is simply a commonwealth by acquisition. Hobbes is setting up two different kinds of commonwealth. Is there any significance to this apparent categorization? We will look for the answer to this question by turning to an examination of sovereignty by acquisition, and with this resolved, pursue the problem of what is meant by lawful industry.

Waynesburg College Library
Waynesburg, Pa. 15370

CHAPTER 5 ☆ HOBBES'S SPECIOUSNESS

OBBES'S theory of human nature leads not necessarily to a justification of naked power, but, on the contrary, serves as the basis of modern libertarian theory. Another notion, given by many commentators as absolute proof of that justification, consists in his "belief" that a sovereign who acquired his rule by force held as much authority, and therefore held his subjects under the same obligation, as a sovereign who acquired his rule by covenant. Indeed, a theory of obligation rooted in force, not consent, has trouble qualifying as legitimate.

In this light, J. Roland Pennock, representing the essence of the view of Hobbes held by many in the past, argued that Hobbes's method, especially his definitions, have led "him occasionally into confusion or inconsistency, and more frequently tends to confuse the reader and so to enable Hobbes to make an unsound conclusion appear sound, by means of specious reasoning. In particular, I shall contend that Hobbes's treatment of liberty (1) leads him into self-contradiction regarding the extent of natural liberty, (2) enables him to argue persuasively but speciously in support of the obligation to obey a sovereign who has attained his position by violence, and (3) prevents him from developing an acceptable theory of political obligation." [1]

Pennock's contentions—that Hobbes contradicted himself in defining the extent of natural liberty and, particularly, that this contradiction prevented him from developing an acceptable theory of political obligation—are without substance. Moreover, while Pennock is correct in seeing that Hobbes argued "speciously in support of the obligation to obey a sovereign who has attained his position by violence," he does not see that Hobbes's reasons for doing so were libertarian. For Hobbes: (1) obligation stems only from voluntary consent or covenant, (2) power can only produce a fact of behavior brought about by coercion, not obligation, and (3) accordingly, there is no obligation simply on the basis of force. It is because power can and does produce a fact that Hobbes moved to his specious argument.

Then, as now, sovereignties created by force or violence existed.[2] Indeed, Hobbes saw that nearly all extant commonwealths originated through conquest rather than compact: "There is scarce a Common-wealth in the world, whose beginnings can in conscience be justified."[3] To champion liberty in those sorts of commonwealth, Hobbes argued, men were obliged to obey the sovereign because in that obedience lay their liberty. For Hobbes, whenever there is obligation there is also the concomitant of obligation— inalienable rights. If sovereigns, even those acquiring rule by force, do not respect the inalienable rights of their subjects, they do not rule by Right, and civil society ceases to exist. Their subjects are not obliged to obey, since they return to a state of nature and are no longer subjects.

Pennock began with Hobbes's discussion of liberty, which he saw as presenting two different definitions for different circumstances, especially for the circumstances of the state of nature and civil society.[4] This in itself involved no inconsistency. In fact, "it can be shown that the two definitions can be reduced, *au fond*, to the same. . . . My point is . . . that both the fact of having two definitions and the particular definitions he chooses contribute to the confusion of Hobbes or his readers or both."[5]

This is a curious statement. After observing that the two can be reduced to the same, he continued to argue that they are yet two different definitions. Therefore, his statement must be construed as meaning: It *can be* shown that the two definitions *can be* reduced to the same, but only speciously. Here Pennock argues from a misunderstanding of both Hobbes's notion of liberty and his notion of will. I shall discuss will, although it is not necessary to the point at hand, since Pennock says his argument stands or falls on the basis of Hobbes's treatment of liberty. Will is not a part of the deliberative process for Hobbes, and Pennock criticizes Hobbes on the basis of what will signifies today. By will Hobbes referred to the end of the deliberative process, the chosen course of action.[6]

Pennock continued by pointing to Hobbes's definition of natural liberty.[7] "In chapter 14 of *Leviathan*, Hobbes defines liberty as 'the absence of external impediments,' or, as he states it in chapter 21, the absence of hindrance to doing whatever man has the will, wit, and ability to do."[8] Pennock infers that Hobbes gave only the external aspect of the definition in chapter 14. Then, in chapter 21, he added to it by applying the external aspect, absence of hindrance, to an internal aspect, doing whatever man has the will[9] or ability to do.

Hobbes, however, gave the same definition in both chapters. He said in chapter 14 that "By LIBERTY, is understood, according to the proper signification of the word, the absence of externall Impediments: which Impediments, may oft take away part of a mans power to do what hee would; but cannot hinder him from using the power left him, according as his judgement, and reason shall dictate to him."[10] A man's power is his means of attaining what he wills. It is his ability. Throughout *Leviathan*, power retained the same meaning. For example, in chapter 21 Hobbes distinguished between a lack of power and a lack of liberty. Observing that when the impediment to motion is found in the constitution of the thing being impeded, it is not because "it wants the Liberty; but the Power to move; as when a stone lyeth still, or a man is fastned to his bed by sicknesse."[11]

Hobbes is pointing to three aspects of man and his condition that must be considered in understanding man's liberty. The first is that the ability to do something must be distinguished from the liberty to accomplish it. If, for example, a man were "prevented" from writing "the great novel of our time" because he was illiterate, ignorant, and possessed the mental ability of a large, grey jellyfish, we would say that it was not the lack of liberty that prevented his writing that novel, but his lack of power.

The second aspect is that man's will must be considered in determining whether his liberty has been curtailed. Earlier Hobbes defined the will as "the last Appetite, or Aversion, immediately adhaering to the action, or to the omission thereof, is that wee call the WILL; the Act, (not the faculty,) of *Willing*."[12] The meaning Hobbes intended to convey is, I believe, misunderstood by Pennock. He said that Hobbes held will as "merely 'the last appetite in deliberating.'"[13] This is only true in part. Hobbes began his paragraph on the will by defining it as the last appetite or aversion. From this statement he moved to an attack upon the scholastic definition of will as solely a "Rationall Appetite." To Hobbes, it was something more. He had already shown it could be a psychological act of aversion. After stating the scholastic definition, he further moved to demonstrate it could also be nonrational appetite, hence the statement it was "*the last Appetite*."[14] This explains the relation of appetite and aversion, but we have yet to see why Hobbes insisted upon the *last* appetite or aversion. To grasp the meaning of will we must first understand what it is to deliberate.

Deliberation is a particular part of the mental process—the determination of choice. When man selects from among alternative objects or courses of action, he deliberates. By way of illustration we may look to the purchase of an automobile. We will ignore the deliberative process involved in arriving at the decision to buy a car and begin with the "will" to seek one out. If upon seeing a particular make or model, the prospective buyer is attracted to it, that attraction relates to appetite. But suppose the dealer wants what is conceived as an exhorbitant amount for the car. The attraction is diminished and the prospective buyer decides not to buy the car. His aversion to the excessive price overcame his appetite for the car. Hobbes would say he willed not to buy the car. Since his choice not to buy the car, his *will* not to, was based upon an aversion to the price and was the direct result of that aversion, Hobbes would call what is in this case an aversion, the will. The last endeavor is the will.

Since deliberation (what today we call the decision-making process) is the mental process of making choice, Hobbes noted there was good reason for calling this process deliberation; "it is a putting an end to the *Liberty* we had of doing, or omitting, according to our own Appetite, or Aversion." [15] Once the decision has been made, then, we have decided to pursue a particular course of action. We no longer have recourse to those other alternatives and thus are not at liberty to pursue them. We *will* a particular course of action. Pennock used deliberation to exemplify the difficulty Hobbes had in holding to his definition of liberty. He quoted Hobbes to the effect that deliberation is so called because it puts an end to the liberty we had of doing or omitting according to our appetites and aversions. His proof is that: "Here he appears to have forgotten about 'external impediments.'"

This provides no proof of inconsistency. Hobbes says explicitly that deliberation puts an end to the liberty we have according to our appetites and aversions. Hobbes does not say it puts an end to the liberty we have in the absence of external impediments. Man's liberty is determined by the absence of external impediments in light of his ability and will. Given an area of liberty, an area with no external obstacles, man can select various courses of action. In casting other alternatives aside, his liberty to pursue them is removed. But this does not deny that his liberty is first determined by the absence of external objects.

Hobbes does not deny choice to man. To him man wills after choice has been made. The selected course of action is what he wills, which is determined by the final appetite or aversion. Practically speaking, therefore, the final appetite or aversion and will are one and the same.

Contrary to Pennock's assertions, [16] Hobbes does not deny man has a faculty of will. But for Hobbes, that faculty is understood in terms of what it is, an activity. To will is to have aversion or appetite for something. With this in mind we can now turn to the relationship between will and liberty.

If an external impediment prevents us from doing what we will (wish) to do, and we have the ability necessary to do it, we may properly say our liberty to do what we will is being restricted. If there is an external impediment to do something we will not to do in the first place, however, we may not say our liberty to do it is being restricted. Given a spaceship, a desire to fly to the moon, and a law that prevents flights to the moon, we may say our liberty to fly to the moon is being restricted. If we have a spaceship, but desire *not* to go to the moon, a law preventing such flights is *not* a restriction on our liberty to go to the moon, since we have already denied ourselves the alternative of going.

The first two aspects of man relating to liberty, the ability and will of man, demonstrate that for Hobbes liberty was a matter of degree. Men with varying kinds and amounts of ability would have varying degrees of liberty. Liberty was further qualified by the aspect of will. The third aspect, external impediment, makes liberty even more a matter of degree.

Although an external impediment may prevent pursuing whatever there is the will and power to pursue, the result is that only a degree of liberty of movement is lost. Using the example of the spaceship, we would see in this instance a man has the power to accomplish what he wills. Suppose, however, that his society has laws that prevent flights to the moon. Those same laws, through their silence, permit individuals to fly to some city with an excellent observatory. Hobbes would say that part of the prospective astronaut's power has been taken away. He is prevented from going to the moon. Yet he still retains some power to do other things he may will. As an alternative he may will to go to the observatory. If so, he exercises a lesser degree of liberty. Obviously the area of freedom has become smaller, for one alternative is removed by the impediment of the law. But the man is still free to choose between remaining alternatives, although he is not at liberty to fly to the moon.

This is what Hobbes meant when he said fear and liberty are consistent.[17] He used the example of a man who, motivated by fear, threw his goods into the sea.[18] Insofar as the man had willed to make the passage safely with his life and his goods, and had been confronted by an external impediment (the sinking ship), his liberty

had been restricted. Thus he was not free to preserve both himself
and his goods. Hobbes was aware that voluntary acts proceeded
only from the will (choice) and therefore if the man did not act
voluntarily (willfully), he was not free.[19]

The number of alternatives open to the man dwindled to sinking
with the ship or throwing his goods overboard. Granted there is
little choice. The fellow can deliberate between death and loss of his
goods, but the point remains; he does have a choice between the
two alternatives. Thus Hobbes could say in throwing his goods
overboard "he doth it neverthelesse very willingly, and may refuse
to doe it if he will: It is therefore the action, of one that was *free*."[20]
This is the meaning Hobbes intended when he wrote, "Impediments, may oft take away part of a mans power to do what hee
would; but cannot hinder him from using the power left him, according as his judgement, and reason shall dictate to him."

To Hobbes, freedom and liberty can be measured only in terms
of degree. Since the merchant had the power and will to make safe
passage, he was not free insofar as the impediment of the sinking
ship prevented him from saving both his life and his goods. But the
area of freedom remaining was the part of his power still in his
possession to save his life. In the choice between insuring his life
on the one hand, or saving his goods and risking death on the other,
he voluntarily chose life. This choice, as noted, is a relatively minute
area of freedom, but it is a degree of freedom, freedom of choice
between two alternatives. Hobbes would not, and did not, say the
merchant is free to choose saving both life and property. An external impediment prevents that. He could, and did, say the man is
free to choose between life and loss of property.

Pennock took Hobbes's notion that liberty is consistent with fear
to mean quite another thing. He continued that: "A man robbed
at gunpoint would be free, according to Hobbes's doctrine. Not
the robber (external), but the fear (internal) constitutes the impediment. If the victim hands over his wallet he is acting voluntarily;
and, for Hobbes, a voluntary action and a free action are one and
the same. . . . Why did Hobbes take this curious position? It seems

unlikely that in his day any more than in ours a man who, for fear of losing his life, allowed a robber to take his money would be generally considered to be free—as free, that is, as the man who was faced with no such hard choice."[21] Hobbes did not, either explicitly or implicitly, say the robber constitutes no external impediment. As we have seen, his statements on the point indicate precisely the opposite. I believe Pennock's error is due primarily to his insistence that liberty is not a matter of degree to Hobbes: "For him, an act is either voluntary or it is not, a man is either obliged or he is not, and he is either free or he is unfree."[22] Pennock's misunderstanding of Hobbes's argument that liberty is consistent with fear, added to his contention that liberty is not a matter of degree to Hobbes, would apply across the board. The fear of the robber, rather than the robber, then could be viewed as the impediment to action. Hobbes's notion that some of a man's power remains in the face of impediments is thereby expanded by Pennock to the notion that *all* of a man's power is either taken away or remains.

From these false premises, Pennock continued: "To speak of actions that are 'freely willed' or 'freely chosen' accordingly makes no sense to Hobbes."[23] Pennock is wrong on this point for several reasons. The first is that, for Hobbes, will occurs after the decision-making process, which is itself deliberation. The second is that Pennock incorrectly views will as the decision-making process. For him, freely willed means what Hobbes meant by freely chosen. Pennock's enclosing "freely willed" and "freely chosen" in quotation marks is in itself mysterious. Had Hobbes actually used the words "freely chosen," quoting them would have made a great deal of sense, as would quoting the words "free choice." A careful examination of Pennock's cited source, however, reveals no mention of "choice."

Free will made no sense to Hobbes, then, since will occurs after free choice has put an end to decision-making. There is another reason Hobbes would deny any meaning to the word. The definition Pennock gave for liberty is Hobbes's definition of a free man, derived from his definition of liberty. "A FREE-MAN, *is he, that in those things, which by his strength and wit he is able to do, is not hindred to doe what he has a will to*."[24] Hobbes then stated it was an error to apply the words "*Free*" or "*Liberty*" to anything but "*Bodies*," for anything not subject to motion is not subject to impediment.[25] Two of the examples he used to demonstrate this contrasted a path's being free with what it means to speak freely. To say that the path is free does not mean the path has liberty, but rather those walking in it have liberty to move along it without being forced to stop. By the same token, speaking freely does not refer to a voice that possesses liberty, but to the man who is free to speak as he will, provided no law prevents it.[26] Hobbes concluded that "from the use of the word *Free-will*, no Liberty can be inferred of the will, desire, or inclination, but the Liberty of the man; which consisteth in this, that he finds no stop, in doing what he has the will, desire, or inclination to doe."[27]

Hobbes required that "free" be applied to the "body." It is in this sense that free choice and free speech, have little meaning; but to choose freely, to speak freely, do have meaning, which is that the man who is speaking or choosing is free to do so. Freely chosen is verbal and relates to the body (man) who is doing the choosing. It is a proper application (Hobbes used it this way: "speak freely"). In this case "freely" modifies the verb that related directly to the body. What Hobbes objected to was the use of "free" adjectivally, modifying a normal activity of the body (choice or speech) so that it became the thing that was free, the body itself.

For Hobbes, liberty or freedom applied to man (or other bodies), not to their activities or faculties. At the same time, he does not deny man has, in our terms, freedom of choice. Further, we have seen that for him liberty was a matter of degree. Liberty depends upon man's will, ability, and the absence of external impediments.

Moreover, Pennock is precisely wrong in his assertion that fear is an "internal impediment." Fear is a form of aversion, "Aversion, with opinion of Hurt."[28] In the case of the robber, the external impediment (the robber) obstructed the victim from continuing along his path and from continuing along his path with his wallet. The victim's area of liberty was reduced to the choice of resisting and perhaps suffering serious injury or handing over his wallet. Any number of aversions or appetites may have been involved in the process of deliberation: desire of ease, courage (an aversion defined as the same as fear but with the hope of avoiding the possible injury by resisting), valor, fear of death.[29] Since the wallet was handed over, we may assume an aversion, fear, was the last passion in deliberation. Accordingly fear is the will. Only voluntary acts proceed from the will. Therefore fear is consistent with a voluntary act, the act of a "free" man.

Fear is not an impediment, as Pennock argued, not even an internal one. It is, in this case, the will and was arrived at through choice. Were Pennock correct in his assertion, there could be no free action. Insofar as man chooses, his choice depends upon various thought. And as these thoughts arrive at a chosen course of action, they, and especially the final thought, constitute impediments. Thus there is no free action or choice. As we have seen, for Hobbes, liberty is determined by the lack of external impediments and by *internal* aspects of man.

And here we arrive at what Pennock sees as the second definition. On the basis of his understanding of Hobbes, he noted that Hobbes moved on to speak of the liberty of subjects. "In this context he recognizes that civil laws, while not really 'external impediments' as previously discussed, are 'artificial chains,' 'made to hold, by the danger, though not by the difficulty of breaking them.'"[30] For Hobbes, the liberty of subjects consisted in those things not forbidden by the law of the state.[31] This is puzzling to Pennock: "Why should Hobbes, in the context of the state, modify the definition of liberty as the absence of external impediments and admit the impediment of fear, which he had so recently ruled out? Apparently he makes exceptions only for the fear of the sovereign. . . . But if a man is free when his action is prompted by fear of a highwayman, why should not the same be true when a policeman provides the motive?"[32]

To solve this "mystery," we must first look to Pennock's belief that, for Hobbes, civil laws are not really external impediments, although they are artificial chains made to hold, not by the difficulty of breaking them, but by the danger of breaking them. Part of Pennock's misunderstanding stems from his belief that Hobbes did not view liberty in terms of degree. Hobbes discussed the liberty of men (and other bodies) prior to his discussion of the liberty of subjects.[33] One might expect Pennock to realize this distinction is a real one, since he saw Hobbes dealt not only with natural liberty but with the liberty of subjects as well. The liberty of men is the liberty man possesses in the state of nature. This is why he is unable to see that the liberty of subjects is less than the liberty of men. Hobbes had argued that the liberty of man depended upon (1) the absence of external impediments, (2) the will to do or wish to do something, and (3) man's ability to do what he willed. Since the existence of law in civil society brings about a great deal of restriction upon man's liberty, the liberty of subjects is of a lesser degree than the liberty of men. There are many more external impediments. But this is not a different definition of liberty.[34]

Another part of the misunderstanding stems from Pennock's belief that Hobbes recognized that civil laws are not really "external impediments." Hobbes makes no statement that substantiates this interpretation. Moreover, since no such statement appears in the material Pennock cited,[35] it must be that Pennock sees that civil laws do not constitute external impediments because they are *instead* "'artificial chains,' 'made to hold, by the danger, though not by the difficulty of breaking them.'"

This interpretation makes meaningful Pennock's question: Why is a man's action free when prompted by fear of a highwayman and not free when prompted by fear of a policeman? The definition of civil law as consisting of artificial chains that derive their strength from the danger involved in breaking them, and not from the difficulty thereof, is equated by Pennock with fear. As was shown earlier, fear is involved. But what Pennock did not see is that the external impediments restrict a degree, rather than the whole, of liberty. We have seen this in the previous discussion of the highwayman. The same is true here. The laws, too, preclude a certain number of alternatives, but man has some left to him. The result is the same.

Furthermore, Pennock does not see wherein fear becomes operative. Hobbes did not say the civil laws derived their strength from the subject's *fear* of breaking them, or even from the subject's *fear of danger* of breaking them. The danger is also an external impediment. I see no reason for Pennock's equation of fear with danger. If the laws do not constitute external impediments, Pennock's interpretation is a little more substantial. If, on the other hand, they do constitute external impediments, his interpretation is even less credible. For when civil law becomes a factor in determining the liberty of subjects, liberty thereby becomes even more a matter of degree.

Pennock was aware that for Hobbes liberty for subjects consists in things not forbidden by the law of the state.[36] This suggests that the liberty of subjects depends upon the lack of external impediments, that is, the silence of the laws. This would make liberty a matter of degree. Hobbes explicitly addressed himself to this point twice. The first reference, in the paragraph entitled "Liberty of Subjects consisteth in Liberty from covenants,"[37] was dismissed by Pennock as simply a treatment of "certain misconceptions that need not concern us here."[38]

Hobbes began by explaining that, at this point, he would speak of the liberty of subjects only as it related to the civil laws.[39] "For seeing there is no Common-wealth in the world, wherein there be Rules enough set down, for the regulating of all the actions, and words of men, (as being a thing impossible:) if followeth necessarily, that in all kinds of actions, by the law praetermitted, men have the Liberty, of doing what their own reasons shall suggest, for the most profitable to themselves. . . . The Liberty of a Subject, lyeth therefore only in those things, which in regulating their actions, the Soveraign hath praetermitted. . . ."[40]

The liberty of subjects depends upon legislation pretermitted. Pennock interpolated this, as well as Hobbes's later statement that "The Greatest Liberty of Subjects, dependeth on the Silence of the Law,"[41] in such a manner as to allow him to change Hobbes's meaning. Pennock interpreted it to mean that not the greatest degree, but all of a subject's liberty depended on the silence of the laws.[42]

Pennock did not understand the profoundly variant degree that liberty held for Hobbes. Rather than seeing that liberty depended upon external circumstance and internal will and ability, Pennock believed Hobbes was inconsistent.

Hobbes also dealt with what he termed the true liberty of a subject. We must recall that this sort of liberty had an exact meaning for Hobbes. True liberty is that which is properly called liberty— natural liberty. This is not the liberty of subjects, it is the liberty of natural man.[43] It is an area not subject to regulation or restriction by civil law. Man, by nature, is in a state of license. Hobbes first reiterated this point: "all men equally, are by Nature Free."[44] Then, building upon the idea of contract, he applied the notion of inalienable rights to a commonwealth. After man enters society he becomes a special sort of man, a subject. He has contracted away certain of his rights to protect other rights, which are inalienable. These inalienable rights are what constitute the true liberty of a subject. They properly equal liberty because they are not subject to restriction. The sovereign may not tamper with them. Thus they are not the equivalent of the liberty of subjects, an area of rights that depends for existence upon the silence of the laws.

They are the rights of nature, that is, the rights of natural man. But man has become a subject. As a subject he enjoys both the liberty stemming from inalienable rights and the liberty stemming from the silence of the laws.[45] There is no specious reasoning in Hobbes's argument on liberty. It is in this argument, however, that

Hobbes's specious reasoning emerges. He argued that the particulars of a subject's true liberty are those things he may refuse to do even though the sovereign (or his laws) command it.[46] Those things he may refuse to do are determined by what rights are transferred in the covenant.[47]

> For in the act of our *Submission*, consisteth both our *Obligation*, and our *Liberty*; which must therefore be inferred by arguments taken from thence; there being no Obligation on any man, which ariseth not from some Act of his own; for all men equally, are by Nature Free. And because such arguments, must either be drawn from the expresse words, *I Authorise all his Actions*, or from the Intention of him that submitteth himselfe to his Power, (which Intention is to be understood by the End for which he so submitteth;) The Obligation, and Liberty of the Subject, is to be derived, either from those Words, (or others equivalent;) or else from the End of the Institution of Soveraignty.[48]

Hobbes appears to be contradicting himself on two points. First, while it is true our obligation stems from our submission, the same does not hold for our liberty. It is true liberty of a subject. Accordingly, this stems from inalienable rights, not from covenant. Hobbes has made both obligation and the liberty of subjects (as respects both true liberty and the ordinary liberty of subjects that is subject to the civil law) dependent upon covenant.

Second, he goes on to say that obligation and liberty can also be derived from something else: the ends for which society was instituted. This means neither obligation nor liberty depend solely upon the voluntary acts of men, as he had previously argued. The end of society is *salus populi*, which was equated with inalienable rights. Thus obligation and liberty exist in any society that creates a condition in which man's activities are characterized by his exercise of the rights to life, liberty, and the pursuit of happiness. Therefore we could say Hobbes argued thusly: (1) voluntary acts aim at one's good; (2) if something benefits man, he voluntarily attempts to attain it; (3) therefore if society pursues the ends for which it was created, man has voluntarily acceded to those ends and thereby submitted to the societal institution.

Hobbes blurred the notions of what man voluntarily does and what he ought voluntarily to do. He does not go the way of Rousseau, however, who insists on a similar basis that man can be forced to be free. Hobbes arrived at this conclusion through specious reasoning. But the results of his conclusion go far beyond Pennock's explanation and stem from a different rationale than does liberty.

Believing Hobbes had worked mental gymnastics with liberty, Pennock attempted to explain the reasons. "Perhaps . . . Hobbes needed to define liberty in this fashion in order to be able later to say that men who covenant to obey a usurping tyrant are bound by their promises."[49] In other words, Hobbes modified his definition of liberty because it enabled him "to argue persuasively but speciously in support of the obligation to obey a sovereign who has attained his position by violence." We have seen that Hobbes did not modify his definition of liberty, and that liberty for him was measured completely in terms of degree. We may disagree with a notion of freedom in which the alternatives are freedom to choose between subservience and death or injury. But this does not mean there is no freedom to choose, unless we take Hobbes at his own word.

In his discussion of inalienable rights, Hobbes argued that man cannot voluntarily do anything that does not aim at some good for himself. He also insisted that a willful act is a voluntary act, and a voluntary act is the act of a man at liberty. I believe it can be argued that a man confronted with the choice of death or a prescribed course of action is not "at liberty" to choose. He cannot voluntarily choose death, for this activity does not aim at his own good. But he is still at liberty, since he voluntarily follows the only course of action left open to him. This is a course wherein he has the will and ability to follow it and no external impediment preventing it. If this is all liberty meant to Hobbes, we would have to agree he is antilibertarian.

But what Pennock failed to see was that this sort of voluntary act ended in the realization not only of obligation, but of liberty, the true liberty of a subject, as well. In his discussion of the true liberty of a subject, Hobbes used his definition of what constituted a voluntary act of man to attribute the consent of men to a sovereignty established by acquisition.[50] Whereas consent is necessary to covenant, and therefore to a justification of obligations, it is also necessary to justify a claim to natural rights. For Hobbes had said whenever there is covenant, a transferring of right, there is also a relational transfer. Man's voluntary acts aim at his own good. He voluntarily transfers right in return for the protection of his inalienable rights. This is the sense in which Hobbes meant liberty depends upon our submission.

We shall see that Hobbes had to admit covenant in a society established by force in order to argue that even in such a society, man must, ought, and does retain his alienable rights. This explains the real speciousness of Hobbes's argument, his assertion that obligation and liberty can be derived from the ends of society. Hobbes's great concern is for the protection of the inalienable rights of man. In his chapter on liberty, Hobbes noted that: "therefore, seeing Soveraignty by Institution, is by Covenant of everyone to everyone; and Soveraignty by Acquisition, by Covenants of the Vanquished to the Victor, or Child to the Parent; It is manifest, that every Subject has Liberty in all those things, the right whereof cannot by Covenant be transferred."[51] Hobbes argued for covenant, established a sovereignty by acquisition to show that man possessed and ought to be able to exercise his inalienable rights, even in that sort of commonwealth.

To understand Hobbes's explanation of sovereignty by acquisition, we must look to his discussion of covenants in chapter 14 of *Leviathan*. "Covenants entred into by fear, in the condition of meer Nature, are obligatory."[52] This throws an entirely different light upon a sovereignty acquired by force. Hobbes applied this notion in his chapter on a commonwealth by acquisition. He defined a commonwealth by acquisition as one in which the sovereign power was acquired by force.[53] This commonwealth came into existence when men, because of fear of death or incarceration, authorized the actions of him or those who held power over their lives and liberty.[54] The only difference Hobbes saw between sovereignty by acquisition and sovereignty by institution was not that one was established through fear and the other was not. Rather, it turned upon who was feared. "And this kind of Dominion, or Soveraignty, differeth from Soveraignty by Institution, onely in this, That men who choose their Soveraign, do it for fear of one another, and not of him whom they Institute: But in this case, they subject themselves, to him they are afraid of. In both cases they do it for fear."[55]

A covenant arrived at through fear is valid in the state of nature. Thus in the case of either kind of commonwealth, man is obligated. Covenants arrived at through fear in civil society, however, are not binding. Once the commonwealth is instituted or acquired, "Promises proceeding from fear of death, or violence, are no Covenants, nor obliging, when the thing promised is contrary to the Lawes."[56] Hobbes is saying here that sovereignty cannot be acquired by force over a commonwealth once formed. For force can destroy the commonwealth, thereby returning its subjects to the state of nature. These remarks are directed to the sovereign who acquires his power by force, whether in the first instance directly from the state of nature, or in the second by first reducing a commonwealth, thereby placing its inhabitants in a state of nature and then acquiring the sovereign power.

Since covenant is involved in either instance, the concomitants, obligation and liberty, also apply. The sovereign may rightfully make laws that do not infringe upon the area of inalienable rights (the ends of society). But he may not infringe upon *those* rights. "The reason is not, because it was made upon fear, but because he that promiseth, hath no right in the thing promised."[57]

CHAPTER 6 ☆ HOBBES'S
"ABSOLUTE" POWER

THE nature of proposals aimed at providing societal stability is determined by what sorts of factors are perceived as the cause of a commonwealth's downfall. Hobbes's view of the nature of those causes resulted in a two-faceted solution. The first, "a Common Power, to keep them in awe, and to direct their actions to the Common Benefit," [1] was directed to subjects as a means of preventing uprisings. In this respect, societal stability requires not only concord and harmony, but coordination as well. To direct the people's actions to the common good is to promote those institutions that insure the "fruits of industry" and that promote knowledge and culture. In the absence of these institutions, life may be protected but there is little assurance of happiness.

The second facet, which is directed to the sovereign, answers the query raised earlier: What made Hobbes believe the sovereign would obey the laws of nature? Hobbes's reasoning was this: If the sovereign is to obey the laws of nature, his own nature must be taken into account. Government must be so constructed as to account for the sovereign's passionate, egoistic nature. [2]

It is interesting to note that while the sovereign must obey the laws of nature, he is morally responsible to God alone. [3] This would seem to rule out any possible obligation from the sovereign to his subjects. Nevertheless, this does not mean subjects could not rightfully rebel against a Prince. For whenever a sovereign violated the area of inalienable rights, he violated the covenant—that which his "Civill Right" (his right to rule) was grounded upon. Since not only his liberty, but also his duty, was similarly grounded, subjects were no longer obligated.

For Hobbes, the dissolution of commonwealths resulted not from "men as they are the *Matter*; but as they are the *Makers*, and orderers of them."[4] Although it is man's passionate nature that excites him to will rebellion,[5] it is an improperly constituted commonwealth that makes rebellion possible. This can be seen in his statement, which opposes natural law and the nature of man. "The Lawes of Nature (as *Justice, Equity, Modesty, Mercy*, and (in summe) *doing to others, as wee would be done to*,) of themselves, without the terrour of some Power, to cause them to be observed, are contrary to the naturall Passions, that carry us to Partiality, Pride, Revenge, and the like."[6] The sovereign's nature does not differ from that of other men; this statement applied to him as well. We will hold in abeyance the implications of this notion in relation to the sovereign. For the present, we are concerned with the implications it holds for subjects: to make subjects obey the laws of nature, there must be power sufficient to excite their fear. In other words, there must be "a Common Power, to keep them in awe, and to direct their actions to the Common Benefit." Such statements have led many astray concerning what Hobbes meant by man's nature and by absolute sovereignty. This is understandable when we look at what he viewed as the primary cause of societal dissolution—the "Want of Absolute Power."[7]

For Hobbes, the greatest cause of instability was the want of absolute power. We have seen such power is not needed to restrain and coerce vicious, savage, bloodthirsty men. We have also seen that this is not the ordinary sort of absolute power. It is restricted to a particular sphere. An area of inalienable rights sets a limit upon the operation of that power.

Yet something about the very words *absolute* and *power* elicits a negative response from most of us. We are conditioned by our culture, and our time, and any association of "absolute" and "power" can be expected to arouse our "aversion."

By way of explication and review, we will look again at a distinction Lee Cameron McDonald drew between Locke and Hobbes in his *Western Political Theory: The Modern Age*: "Here is the crux of the distinction between Locke and Hobbes or even Filmer. For the latter two, the need for power or the fact of power was its justification; for Locke, the subject's consent was its justification."[8] This evaluation of the Hobbes-Locke distinction appears to ignore, or to discard, some of the most significant Hobbesian observations on the problem of obligation. Therefore, we must ask, first, does McDonald mean by "justification" power's right to exist, or its right to be obeyed? Second, is he inferring in the statement that there is no significant difference between the need for power and the fact of power? In the answer to such questions, the real (or fundamental) distinction between Hobbes and Locke will be found. For example, it seems quite true that the need for power, properly understood, is the justification for the existence of power. For Hobbes, power exists because it is necessary to the preservation of order—which in turn is necessary to the fundamental natural law and its concomitant natural rights (or vice versa). This is, of course, to say that a man is obliged by his nature to preserve himself— otherwise he ceases to exist; and he obviously, therefore, has a right to preserve himself.

But to say that the need for power is the justification for its existence suggests two things: that power needs justification, and that power comes into being in answer to a need. Now while the latter does not necessarily imply anything except that the accumulation of power comes about as a result of some natural process that proceeds accidentally in relation to an equally accidental development of need, for Hobbes, such accidental accumulations of power are characteristic primarily of the state of nature; and they are represented by the several instances in primitive society of men banding together in transient, *ad hoc* combinations. But the overwhelming fact about such power is that it is inadequate for the ends that gave it birth. It is not sufficient for the protection of the individual in the exercise of his natural rights to self-preservation, liberty, and happiness.

What is required for that end is absolute power. If Hobbes is to be given his due, it is essential that a clear distinction be made between absolute power and totalitarian power. It is this distinction that preserves and makes understandable the essentially liberal quality of Hobbes's thinking and of his system. Absolute power, which is properly understood as absolute only within the sphere of its rightful exercise, is indeed justified by need—by the fact that it is absolutely essential for the protection of the individual in the exercise of his natural right to self-preservation. No power that is not absolute at the point of application, in other words, in any situation that calls into being a need for the exercise of power, is sufficient to attain the desired end.[9]

The significant fact about absolute power is that it is a purely political phenomenon. But the need for absolute power is equally as evident in the state of nature as it is in civil society (or the civil state). That is, it is logically evident in either situation. It is only as that need becomes evident experientially, however, that the power becomes a possibility. It is the natural result of man's exercise of his natural rights that finally makes obvious the need, which thereby results in the making of the covenant. And it is the covenant that both creates and authorizes absolute power.

Whatever difficulties could be involved in Hobbes's working out the implications of this fact, thus far his system reflects the twofold observation that although absolute power is necessary, it is naturally impossible. Its existence is impossible in the state of nature for the quite simple, but extremely important, reason that absolute power is not a natural phenomenon. It requires convention for its existence. As Hobbes pointedly observed, there is no such thing as absolute physical (that is, natural) power. The people, conceived of as existing in some degree in a self-conscious group, are undoubtedly always capable of a successful revolution. So perhaps the above statement should be amended to read: no absolute physical power except that which is exercised by the strongest physical force. Since the sovereign cannot be thought of ultimately as the most powerful physical force in a society, it follows that insofar as his power is absolute, it is absolute by consent. It is absolute by virtue of the fact that each has covenanted with every other to submit every one of themselves to the exercise of absolute power by the sovereign.

It is in this sense, then, that absolute power is a conventional, or artificial, phenomenon rather than a natural one. And it is because absolute power can be realized only through convention that the covenant and resulting Leviathan come into existence. But if this is the case, how is it possible to suppose that in Hobbes's system it is the "need or the fact of power" that justifies power? In the Hobbesian context, *need* and *fact* are literally worlds apart. They are so far apart in significance they hardly can be treated the way McDonald treats them. And what is more, McDonald's use of the word *justification* is quite ambiguous.

It would seem proper to agree with McDonald's formulation to this extent: The creation of absolute power is justified by the need for absolute power. This is to say that the people are justified in submitting themselves to the exercise of absolute power by the sovereign because it has become obvious such power is necessary for the exercise of their natural rights. But while the implication of obligation is surely present in such a formulation, it is really a separate proposition that defines the relationship between the citizen and the power he has helped to create. He is obligated to the sovereign not because the sovereign exists, nor simply because there is a need for the sovereign. His obligation to obey, in Hobbes's view, is not completely divorced either from the need for absolute power or from the fact of its existence; and this must be recognized. But the crucial, the absolutely central, thing is neither the need, nor the fact of absolute power. Rather, it is that absolute power had to be created to attain the ends of society and that essential to the process of creation was the promise of each to submit.

Obviously Locke would never have accused Hobbes of having no basis for obligation since he wrote: "And thus every Man, by consenting with others to make one Body Politick under one Government, puts himself under Obligation to everyone of that Society, to submit to the determination of the *majority*, and to be concluded by it; or else this *original Compact*, whereby he with others incorporates into *one Society*, would signifie nothing, and be no Compact, if he be left free, and under no other ties, than he was in before in the State of Nature" (sec. 97). Substituting "sovereign" for "the majority" makes this a perfectly respectable Hobbesian quote.

Hobbes meant two things by "absolute power." First, authority of power must be sufficient to attain the ends for which men enter civil society. This relates to the quantity of power Hobbes saw as necessary or absolute. Second, and more central to the meaning, authorized power must be held absolutely, that is, it must not be divided. Division of powers in this sense relates to mixed government, not separation of powers. For Hobbes makes clear he would not object to a separation of powers within certain limits.

To arrive at an understanding of the first aspect of Hobbes's meaning, we must recall that sovereign power derives from the power of all particular members. Through covenant, every man transfers part of his power to the sovereign. Hobbes was sophisticated enough to know that power cannot be transferred in the manner of filling a pail from several smaller glasses. The transfer of power from each particular man to a sovereign, thereby establishing sovereign power, is realized when "each citizen hath conveyed all his strength and power to that man or council; which to have done (because no man can transfer his power in a natural manner) is nothing else than to have parted with his right of resisting." [10] Since man does not transfer *all* his rights, retaining his inalienable rights, in the first instance this absolute power is absolute only within a particular sphere.

But that it is absolute within its proper sphere there can be no doubt. This power "is as great, as possibly men can be imagined to make it." [11] Under the title "*Right to the End, Containeth Right to the Means,*" Hobbes made an interesting argument on the notion of power. "They that give to a man the Right of government in Soveraignty, are understood to give him the right of levying money to maintain Souldiers; and of appointing Magistrates for the administration of Justice."[12] The sovereign also "by right hath as great a power over each single citizen, as each man hath over himself considered out of that civil state, that is, supreme and absolute, to be limited only by the strength and forces of the city itself, and by nothing else in the world."[13] Power must be "perfect enough" to attain the ends of society.[14] It is perfect enough when sufficient to form the wills of all to peace, defense, and the common benefit. Absolute power must be of this quantity.

Are there limits upon this power? The only limit, keeping in mind that it is already restricted to its proper sphere, is man's ability to create absolute power through artificial means. This brings us to the nub of Hobbes's meaning. To remain absolute, power must not be limited. "For Power Unlimited, is absolute soveraignty."[15]

What is limited power? For Hobbes, it is mixed government. Hobbes saw that most men would agree government ought not be divided.[16] Most also would agree, however, that it ought to be moderated and bounded by limits.[17] Hobbes agreed with both points. He believed it was reasonable to moderate government.

> But if these men, when they speak of moderating and limiting, do understand dividing it, they make a very fond distinction. Truly, for my part, I wish that not only Kings, but all other persons endued with supreme authority, would so temper themselves as to commit no wrong, and only minding their charges, contain themselves within the limits of the natural and divine laws. But they who distinguish thus, they would have the chief power bounded and restrained by others; which, because it cannot be done, but that they who do set the limits must needs have some part of the power, whereby they may be enabled to do it, the government is properly divided, not moderated.[18]

There was one problem. To moderate or limit power was to divide it, thereby opening a Pandora's box. The two principles, one of moderation or limitation, and one of undivided government, were antipathetic. Hobbes is speaking here of division between monarchic, aristocratic, and democratic bodies, not of a separation of powers within either form. In example after example the notion that powers divided mutually destroy one another[19] was related only to a division between monarchic, aristocratic, or democratic parts.[20]

Representative of these examples is Hobbes's argument in chapter 18 of *Leviathan*. He noted that if the sovereign transferred the power of the militia, he retained judicial power in vain since he could not enforce the laws. Or if he gave away the power of raising money, the power of the militia is retained in vain.[21] It is in this kind of division "whereof it is said, *a Kingdome divided in it selfe cannot stand*: For unlesse this division precede, division into opposite Armies can never happen. If there had not first been an opinion received of the greatest part of *England*, that these Powers were divided between the King, and the Lords, and the House of Commons, the people had never been divided, and fallen into this Civill Warre."[22]

The most telling example occurs in his discussion of mixed government where Hobbes noted

> that such government, is not government, but division of the Common-wealth into three Factions, and call it mixt Monarchy; yet the truth is, that it is not one independent Commonwealth, but three independent Factions; nor one Representative Person, but three. In the Kingdome of God, there may be three Persons independent, without breach of unity in God that Reigneth; but where men Reigne, that be subject to diversity of opinions, it cannot be so. And therefore if the King bear the person of the People, and the generall Assembly bear also the person of the People, and another Assembly bear the person of a Part of the people, they are not one Person, nor one Soveraign, but three Persons, and three Soveraigns.[23]

This does not apply solely to the monarchic form. Hobbes says his discussion of sovereignty is to be understood in terms of the abstract. "I speak not of the men, but (in the Abstract) of the Seat of Power." [24] There are certain powers involved in sovereignty regardless "in what Man, or Assembly of men, the Sovaraign Power is placed, and resideth." [25] And all forms of government "must have the Sovaraign Power . . . entire." [26] We find that in the de facto situation all do have the same absolute power. [27]

But what of separation of powers? In light of Hobbes's discussion we might believe a separation would be a division. The answer lies in seeing that Hobbes is discussing both sovereign power and the right thereto. Hobbes did not object to a separation between the *right* to power and the *exercise* of that power. His concern was that one man, or assembly, must retain the *right* to power. [28] As long as this was accepted, any number of men could exercise it. Separation of powers, therefore, would be consistent in any form of government, even a mixed form, if the exercise, and not the right, were separated. However, Hobbes would argue, mixed government is not possible without a separation of right. He argued, moreover, that limited government, on the basis of an aristocratic or democratic part limiting a monarch (or however), was impossible. The part that limited the other was, for Hobbes, actually the predominate power, that is, the sovereign. [29] It is a separation of powers (which is to say the exercise of power) within any unmixed form of government that is both possible and permissible.

Summing up Hobbes's statements about absolute power, we see there are five aspects of sovereign power: (1) it is absolute within its proper sphere; (2) it is as great as men can make it; (3) it is not to be limited (which means divided) and therefore there should be no mixed government; (4) the exercise of it can be separated, but not the right; and (5) it is the same (in terms of quantity and quality) in *all* forms of government, monarchy, aristocracy, and popular.

Hobbes's solution to the problem of instability caused by subjects was power, absolute power. Since the sovereign, whether a man, or men, is subject to the same passions as all men, why did Hobbes believe the sovereign would exercise power only within its proper sphere? To answer this question we must turn to Hobbes's choice of monarchy as the best form of government. We do this with one thing in mind. His selection could not have been based upon power considerations. "The difference between these three kindes of Common-wealth, consisteth not in the difference of Power; but in the difference of Convenience, or Aptitude to produce the Peace, and Security of the people; for which end they were instituted."[30] This statement provides a key to understanding Hobbes's teaching. The key is found in the words *power* and *convenience*. Hobbes's argument throughout his works concerned the solution to the problem resulting from the "want of power." But now we are jarred by his statement that power is not all that is necessary. This is beyond doubt one of the most crucial passages in *Leviathan*.

The difference between monarchy and the other forms of government is monarchy's "convenience" to produce the peace and security of the people. This is a beforehand letter to his critics, showing that the security he seeks is not simply the absence of war, nor a simple preservation of life. This statement shows that "peace" is not equatable to "the security of the people." It is the peace, *and* security of the people. The role of power in Hobbes's system is simply this: achieving the peace, thereby making possible the condition necessary for producing the security of the people. The latter end of society encompasses the former, and peace is a prerequisite to *salus populi*. By determining the convenience of monarchy to *salus populi* we grasp, at the same time, Hobbes's great insight into man.

Hobbes gives four reasons why a monarchy is more "convenient" than aristocracy and democracy. He also denies two asserted inconveniences of monarchy. Turning first to this denial, we find an aid in ascertaining the meaning of those four reasons. Hobbes wrote that "to say there is inconvenience, in putting the use of the Soveraign Power, into the hand of a Man, or an Assembly of men; is to say that all Government is more Inconvenient, than Confusion, and Civill Warre."[31] The effect of this statement is that he denied the advantage of monarchy over aristocracy and democracy found in the second, third, and fourth reasons, since those three reasons are based upon confusion and war.[32]

There is some significance in the fact that it is listed *first*. There is greater significance in the fact that the fundamental tenets of Hobbes's entire teaching are found in germ within this single paragraph: the nature of man, sovereignty, and the ends of society.[33]

He began by noting that a man, whether monarch or of the assembly, who is sovereign bears two persons, one public, the other private.[34] No matter how careful he is to procure the common interest, he is no less careful to procure the private good for himself.[35] "And for the most part, if the publique interest chance to crosse the private, he preferrs the private: for the Passions of men, are commonly more potent than their Reason. From whence it follows, that where the publique and private interest are more closely united there is the publique most advanced."[36] Hobbes supported monarchy because only within this form of government do we find the sovereign's "private interest is the same with the publique."[37] This is the reason a monarch would exercise power only within his proper sphere. "The riches, power, and honour of a Monarch arise onely from the riches, strength and reputation of his Subjects. For no King can be rich, nor glorious, nor secure; whose Subjects are either poore, or contemptible, or too weak through want, or dissention, to maintain a war against their enemies."[38] Hobbes rejected democracy and aristocracy because the public prosperity did not come together as much with the private fortune of one who is "corrupt or ambitious" in those forms of government. On the other hand, corruption and ambition in a monarch lead to the attainment of the public prosperity.[39] But corruption and ambition in members of an assembly lead to "many times a perfidious advice, a treacherous action, or a Civill warre."[40]

One of Hobbes's greatest contributions to the American Founding Fathers is the notion of attaining the public good through the pursuit of private interest. It is, at the same time, his reason for choosing monarchy, for believing a monarch would not transgress upon inalienable rights, for believing that he would exercise power only within its proper sphere, and for believing he would attain the ends of society.

Two underlying libertarian principles modified even sovereignty by acquisition, thereby further extending liberty. The first was Hobbes's specious argument on the right to rights. Previously, he had based that right upon a natural condition of rights and a notion of inalienable rights. He changed positions to base it upon the covenant. In attributing obligation of citizens to a sovereign who acquired his power by force, he was also able to inject the inalienable rights of man into a sovereignty by acquisition.

The second principle is this. Hobbes's notion of attaining the public good through the pursuit of private interest works the same in a sovereignty acquired by acquisition as by institution. Its feasibility depends not upon the manner in which society is instituted, nor upon the natural law, nor upon a society's stated ends. It is based upon the nature of man, passionate man: even corrupt ambitious man. If any criticism upon this point can be made from within Hobbes's system, it seems to me to be this: monarchs can be rich, glorious, secure, and powerful if most of their subjects are poor and only a few have a great deal of wealth; the single thing that would not result would be honor. To give Hobbes his due, we must recognize that honor is, perhaps, of the most weight. The single passion mentioned specifically in this paragraph is ambition. And we must agree that a monarch would be ambitious, especially if he acquired his position through force.

As Hobbes presents them, honor and ambition go hand in hand, and rightly so. Ambition is "Desire of Office, or precedence."[41] To honor a man is to value him at a high rate.[42] Those who desire honor are ruled by two passions, both of which are a form of joy.[43] These are the love of praise and fame.[44] While these appear as the *desire* of fame and the *desire* of praise, Hobbes also wrote, "That which men Desire, they are also sayd to LOVE."[45] Praise is "the forme of Speech whereby men signifie their opinion of the Goodnesse of any thing."[46] Fame is the hope of praise after death.[47]

The effect of these desires is that "Desire [love] of Praise, disposeth to laudable actions. . . . Desire [love] of Fame after death does the same."[48] The reason Hobbes thought fame similar in effect was that although men have no "sense" of the praise given them after death, they still may derive "a present delight therein, from the foresight of it, and of the benefit that may redound thereby to their posterity."[49]

Hobbes could say ambitious men want wealth, honor, fame, and praise, if for no other reason than that he led us to this conclusion by prudent definition. I believe, however, as did he, this *is* true. At any rate, we have seen that Hobbes offered a twofold solution to the problem of societal instability. His solution does reflect the nature of man, but it is a reflection of a passionate man, not of a savage, bloodthirsty, vicious-natured man. We will now turn to the "author" who spoke of men as ambitious, rapacious, and vindictive—Publius.

CHAPTER 7 ☆ THE FEDERALIST:
FROM THE TRUTH OF SPECULATION TO
THE UTILITY OF PRACTICE

"In a way beset with those that contend, on one side for too great Liberty, and on the other side for too much Authority, 'tis hard to passe between the points of both unwounded. . . .[1] I recover some hope, that one time or other, this writing of mine, may fall into the hands of a Sovereign, who will consider it himselfe, (for it is short, and I think clear,) without the help of any interessed, or envious Interpreter; and by the exercise of entire Soveraignty, in protecting the Publique teaching of it, convert this Truth of Speculation, into the Utility of Practice."[2]

The Federalist was first published as a series of papers in the New York City press. As Martin Diamond observed, they were addressed to three different audiences: the people of the state of New York, the delegates at the state ratifying conventions, and posterity.[3] Concerning the latter audience, Diamond wrote: "It seems clear that its authors also looked beyond the immediate struggle and wrote with a view to influencing later generations by making their work the authoritative commentary on the meaning of the Constitution. While *The Federalist* was the most immediate kind of political work, a piece of campaign propaganda, it spoke also to thoughtful men then and now, with a view to the permanence of its argument."[4]

With these two statements Diamond made a transition to an element he had not yet covered. Whereas the first statement points out that *The Federalist* could influence later generations because of its authoritative commentary on the meaning of the Constitution, the second statement speaks of the permanence of the argument in these papers. And here is an important point. The permanency of an argument turns upon underlying principles of politics, as well as authoritative exposition.

Diamond further noted that the authors did not have to deal "*primarily* . . . with the most controversial subject, namely, the standard by which they themselves deemed the Constitution good."[5] It is only on a secondary basis that, while going "very far," Hamilton and Madison suggested "the theoretical grounds upon which a wise acceptance of the Constitution should rest."[6] Whereas this could maintain consistency for Publius by not making Hamilton and Madison "lay bare their ultimate differences," at the same time, it explains "why *The Federalist* falls short of those great works in which theoretical matters are pressed to their proper, that is, farthest limits."[7]

If we return for a moment to the "great" works of Hobbes and Locke, we may recall that when pressed to their farthest limits, they exhibit very serious problems. Locke said that the majority ought to conclude the community. The majority ought to determine the standards of right and wrong. Yet the executive ought to employ the prerogative, even when contrary to those standards determined by the majority. The only "appeal" was the sword. Hobbes, on the other hand, believed liberty rarely would be threatened by a monarch, since it was in the monarch's private interest to protect liberty. At the same time he knew there were and would be princes who would not protect or recognize men's "unalienable rights." His solution is precisely the same as Locke's. When the sovereign did not honor the law of nature, the obligation of subjects ceased, returning all to a state of nature and concomitant state of war.

I disagree with Diamond to this extent. I believe *The Federalist* ranks with at least the "great" works of Hobbes and Locke. Publius, working from a similar view of the nature of man, overcame both problems through a solution that was consistent with liberty. Hobbes's greatest shortcoming was his failure to see that a monarch need not nurture the strength and wealth of all members to be glorious, powerful, wealthy, and famous. For what he forgot was one of his own principles. While praise, and therefore fame, "disposeth to laudable actions," they are very particular actions, being "such as please them whose judgement they value: for of those men we contemn, we contemn also the Praises." The monarch in the society of Hobbes's day would be much more likely to be indifferent to the poor than to the wealthy, to the weak than to the strong, to the many than to the few. When this notion is added to that demonstrated above (a king can be wealthy and powerful if some have a great deal of wealth and others very little) we see little protection for the majority of the commonwealth.

I believe Locke attempted to overcome this problem through "majority rule." In so doing, he was confronted with the problem of the majority faction. But I believe his point is well taken. If there must be within society some who are favored, let it be the majority rather than an absolute monarch and his chosen few.

I know the so-called brief for majority rule as a form of government is *very* questionable in the *Second Treatise*. But certainly the principle is there. I am also certain it can be argued that the majority Locke is writing about is not a majority of numbers, but rather of wealth and position. Even if this were true, however, I think it would amount to a poor criticism of Locke, who wrote during a time when less than 2 percent of the adult population were "represented people." At any rate, Locke's solution to the problem of majority (by either definition) faction resulted in a return to the state of nature and the state of war. Neither a tyrannical majority, nor executive prerogative, nor war, as a means of ultimate "value allocation," can be considered a part of our constitutional system.

I intend to show through *The Federalist* that the Constitution employed Hobbes's solution in a manner that both resolved the problem of instability (without resorting to the arms of monarchy) and secured men's rights. Publius's solution is simply this: a constitutional system that employs the pursuit of private interest to attain the public good. But where Hobbes applied this principle only to government, the genesis of our heritage lies in the fact that Publius applied it to society as well, thereby enlarging, refining, and correcting Hobbes's teaching so it could be "converted into the Utility of Practice." If the theoretical principles of *The Federalist* fall short because they do not go far enough, the things they fall short of are also the shortcomings of Hobbes and Locke. There is at least one element common to all three. There is no difference between their views of human nature.

Publius also viewed man's nature as passionate. Striking a Hobbesian note he asked, "What is government itself, but the greatest of all reflections on human nature?"[8] "Men are ambitious, vindictive, and rapacious."[9] Thus "Ambition, avarice, personal animosity, party opposition, and many other motives not more laudable than these, are apt to operate . . . upon those who support as those who oppose the right side of a question."[10] As with those on both sides of a question, passions operate upon the governed and governors alike. Publius appealed to the governed that they might not allow the "sacred knot" of union to "be severed or dissolved by ambition or by avarice, by jealousy or misrepresentation."[11] He showed his concern that even a President might "sacrifice his duty to his interest" because of avarice or ambition.[12]

His awareness of a sweeping variety of passions, ambition, avarice, conceit, envy, fear, jealousy, love of fame, love of novelty, pride, resentment, self-love, et cetera,[13] and of their effects, is found throughout the papers. For Publius, or Hobbes, government must reflect man's nature. If the cause of instability is due to man as the maker of commonwealths, and not as the matter, to overcome that cause is to rightly order the commonwealth so it accounts for man as the matter.

For Hobbes there was a science of politics[14] so that "The skill of making, and maintaining Common-wealths, consisteth in certain Rules."[15] Publius also believed there was a science of politics.[16] He saw, moreover, the efficacy of various principles: separation of powers, legislative checks and balances, judges holding office during good behavior, and legislative representatives elected by the

Waynesburg College Library
Waynesburg, Pa. 15370

people.[17] By employing these accepted principles along with two additional, "novel" principles, Publius believed he had attained the right ordering of society. The two novel principles are first the enlargement of the orbit,[18] thereby helping create the second, a proliferation of interests.[19] We turn now to an examination of that rightly ordered society, the causes of instability, and the means whereby those causes tend to be mitigated.

The form of government determines the particular sort of problems that will cause the most concern in a particular society. Given a majority-rule form of government, Locke had to contend primarily with the majority faction. His solution was the prerogative, and thereby the arms, of the executor. A secondary concern was the protection of the rights of the people, determined by the nature of government. Hobbes's thorniest problem concerned his search for a means of protecting individual rights. He effectively ruled out the problem of faction by giving the right of sovereignty to a monarch and making that power absolute within the limits of the covenant and therefore the laws of nature. But with this sort of power little could prevent a monarch from violating the contract.

What form of government determined the primary problem Publius faced? In noting that observations correctly attributed to democratic forms of government were incorrectly applied to republican forms,[20] Publius made clear which form determined the primary problem he faced. He spoke first of "The error which limits republican government to a narrow district."[21] Further, "the vices and defects of the republican" form had been meretriciously demonstrated by "citing as specimens . . . the turbulent democracies of ancient Greece and modern Italy."[22] Thus through a confusion of names, observations applicable to a democracy had been transferred to a republic.[23]

> Such a fallacy may have been the less perceived, as most of the popular governments of antiquity were of the democratic species; and even in modern Europe, to which we owe the great principle of representation, no example is seen of a gov-

ernment wholly popular, and founded, at the same time, wholly on that principle. If Europe has the merit of discovering this great mechanical power in government, by the simple agency of which the will of the largest political body may be concentred, and its force directed to any object which the public good requires, America can claim the merit of making the discovery the basis of unmixed and extensive republics.[24]

Publius argued two points. First, he proved that application of the representative principle to a democratic form of government allows extensive republics. And second, since the representative principle does allow an extensive republic, upon a democratic basis, it allows an unmixed republic. As Diamond observed, "The word 'unmixed' must be read in its full force. The American states were not *mixed regimes* [but] wholly popular states."[25] Publius saw no examples of government in Europe based wholly upon the representative system and, at the same time, wholly popular.

Democracy and the American republic are both wholly popular, but only the American republic is further based upon the representative principle. Publius had twice before defined democracy and republic. He first dealt with "a pure democracy, by which I mean a society consisting of a small number of citizens, who assemble and administer the government in person."[26] A republic, on the other hand, is "a government in which the scheme of representation takes place."[27] Later, he added "The true distinction between these forms . . . is, that in a democracy, the people meet and exercise the government in person; in a republic, they assemble and administer it by their representatives and agents."[28]

A republic and a democracy differ in that the latter is pure, and by implication, the former is impure. However, the strand of impurity results not from mixing in elements from other forms of government. A democratic republic is a wholly popular government. It differs only from pure democracy in that representation takes place. Thus *The Federalist*'s republic, as democracy, is a species of the genus, popular government.[29]

Since Publius espoused popular government, the primary problem confronting him was "to break and control the violence of faction."[30] "The friend of popular governments never finds himself so much alarmed for their character and fate, as when he contemplates their propensity to this dangerous vice. He will not fail, therefore, to set a due value on any plan which, without violating the principles to which he is attached, provides a proper cure for it."[31] The friend of popular government will set a due value on any plan that provides a proper cure while not violating the principles to which he is attached, among which is popular government. The task Publius set for himself was "To secure the public good and private rights against the danger of . . . faction, and at the same time to preserve the spirit and form of popular government."[32] This is, as "G. L. Pierson applied to Tocqueville, to 'make democracy safe for the world.'"[33]

For Publius, the effects of faction were what they had been historically. "The instability, injustice, and confusion introduced into the public councils, have, in truth, been the mortal diseases under which popular governments have everywhere perished."[34] "Complaints are everywhere heard . . . that our governments are too unstable, that the public good is disregarded in the conflicts of rival parties."[35] And greatly important to Publius was the problem Locke faced: "Measures are too often decided, not according to justice and the rights of the minor party, but by the superior force of an interested and overbearing majority."[36] The "heaviest misfortunes . . . must be chiefly, if not wholly, effects of the unsteadiness and injustice with which a factious spirit has tainted our public administrations."[37]

The primary source of Publius's concern was the problem of faction, since "the whole power of the proposed government is to be in the hands of the representatives of the people."[38] A faction is: "a number of citizens, whether amounting to a majority or minority of the whole, who are united and actuated by some common impulse of passion, or of interest, adverse to the rights of other citizens, or to the permanent and aggregate interests of the community."[39] Publius saw two methods of "curing the mischiefs" of faction: by removing its causes, or by controlling its effects.[40] There are two means of removing the causes of faction: by destroying liberty which nurtures it, or by giving the same opinions, passions, and interests to all.[41] But to destroy liberty is worse than the disease. Whereas this is unwise, the second means of removing the causes is impracticable. For "as long as the reason of man continues fallible, and he is at liberty to exercise it, different opinions will be formed. As long as the connection subsists between his reason and his self-love, his opinions and his passions will have a reciprocal influence on each other; and the former will be objects to which the latter will attach themselves. The diversity in the faculties of men, from which the rights of property originate, is not less an insuperable obstacle to a uniformity of interests."[42]

There are at least two "insuperable obstacles" to a uniformity of interests. The first stems from man's reason and passions. Reason, as well as passion, is apt to operate upon those on both sides of a question. Man is subject to error. Therefore, through reasoning, men will arrive at different opinions about things. This difference may be widened because these opinions are also determined in part by passions. Opinions and passions influence one another, and opinions are objects to which passions attach themselves.

Different opinions result from reason *and* passion. But this is not to say different opinions result from man's *reason*. Differences of opinion result from "fallible" reason. I believe that Publius sees the possibility of truth stemming from reason, which on a particular issue, or at a particular time, is not fallible. But for infallibility to occur, man's passions must either be in accord with truth or must be suspended. Man's passionate nature rules out the latter, leaving the only possible explanation that passion can be compatible with reason in arriving at the truth of the matter.

The second obstacle is the diversity in the faculties of men from which the rights of property originate. Madison made a crucial observation on this point. Not protection of the rights of property, but "The protection of these faculties is the first object of government."[43] For it is the protection of different and unequal faculties of acquiring property that allows various degrees and kinds of property to be held by man.[44] And "from the influence of these on the sentiments and views of the respective proprietors, ensues a division of the society into different interests and parties."[45] Both amounts of property and kinds of property influence the sentiments and views of men. The opinions men hold due either to their degree or kind of property create one of the sources of interests and parties, that is, of faction.

The irony of Publius's government is that in protecting the varying faculties of man, it protects the aspect of man that causes faction. Such things as freedom of thought, so necessary for those with a flair for creativity, allow variable expression by men, and in great part, ensure their liberty to do or think as they please within the limits of the law. The lawful acquisition of property, based upon men's faculties for doing so, elicits a division of the society into different interests and parties.

Since it is differences in the faculties of men that cause divisions within society, Publius continued that "The latent causes of faction are thus sown in the nature of man; and we see them everywhere brought into different degrees of activity, according to the different circumstances of civil society."[46] The nature of man also causes factions based upon interests other than property. Opinions about religion, government, and different leaders have "divided mankind into different parties" and "inflamed them with mutual animosity."[47] In fact, "So strong is this propensity of mankind to fall into mutual animosities, that where no substantial occasion presents itself, the most frivolous and fanciful distinctions have been sufficient to kindle their unfriendly passions and excite their most violent conflicts."[48]

A civil war in England fought over which end of the church to place the altar in bore sufficient testimony for Publius's point (as it had for Hobbes's). History served to demonstrate the effect of factions stemming from different opinions regarding government, religion, and various leaders.[49] "But the most common and durable source of factions has been the various and unequal distribution of property. Those who hold and those who are without property have ever formed distinct interests in society. Those who are creditors, and those who are debtors, fall under a like discrimination. A landed interest, a manufacturing interest, a mercantile interest, a moneyed interest, with many lesser interests, grow up of necessity in civilized nations, and divide them into different classes, actuated by different sentiments and views." [50]

The most common source of faction has been the various and unequal distribution of property. Publius is obviously implying here that it continued to cause factions until he tackled it. And we must permit a certain pride he manifests when further noting that it *has been* the most durable source, that is, the source most difficult to overcome and control. The amount and the kind of property have been the most frequent causes of faction throughout history and the most difficult to overcome.

As examples of the two sorts of division resulting from causes based on kind and amount of property, Publius listed: have-nots divided from haves, creditors divided from debtors, a landed interest, a manufacturing interest, a mercantile interest, a monied interest, wherein all are divided from the rest. The haves and have-nots are clearly factions caused by amount of property. The latter four are clearly factions caused by kind of property. But what of the creditors and debtors? They seem to be caused by amount of property. That is, they do until we take a closer look at the debtor class. In a commercial society, the property owners are usually those who owe the most money. Mark Twain summed this up in *The Gilded Age*, wherein one of his characters boasted of how he had come to New York a few years before, penniless, and shortly became a big success. He *owed* a million dollars. At any rate, some of the wealthy are debtors and do not fall neatly into the amount category, which would be necessary if we were to align wealthy creditors against non-wealthy and debtors.

Publius tells us that "The regulation of these various and interfering interests forms the task of modern legislation, and involves the spirit of party and faction in the necessary and ordinary operations of the government."[51] Hereby he raised both the problem *for* government and the problem *of* government, given a popular form. The task of regulating these interests falls upon the legislature. But the legislature is nothing more than a representation of those interests within society. At this point, he faced the same problem Hobbes and Locke faced. "No man is allowed to be a judge in his own case, because his interest would certainly bias his judgment, and, not improbably, corrupt his integrity."[52]

Hobbes thought he solved the problem by giving the judicial power to one man, the monarch. And when it came to a problem of the monarch judging in his own cause, Hobbes believed the monarch's cause was the same as the public good. There was no problem here. Locke, on the other hand, spoke in terms of a "common judge." The majority concluded the minority, and determined the standards of right and wrong. Whether the laws, the majority, the legislature, or the executor, or all can be said to be the common judge is not clear in Locke when the majority is opposed by the prerogative. If it is the majority, the prerogative of the executive seemingly prevents judging in their own cause. But this solution is as insufficient as Hobbes's seems.

Whereas Hobbes and Locke insisted men ought not be judges in their own cause, Publius gave a different answer. "The parties are, and must be, themselves the judges."[53] His reasoning was that many legislative acts are judicial determinations concerning the rights of large bodies of citizens. "And what are the different classes of legislators but advocates and parties to the causes which they determine?"[54]

"Justice ought to hold the balance between them."[55] It ought to hold the balance between competing interests, but when the parties are judges, "the most numerous party, or, in other words, the most powerful faction must be expected to prevail."[56] It is too much to expect "enlightened statesmen" to adjust these clashes and bring them into line with the public good; such men will not always be found. Besides, in most cases these interests cannot be brought into

accord with the public good without looking to "indirect and re-
mote considerations."[57] Such considerations "will rarely prevail
over the immediate interests which one party may find in disregard-
ing the rights of another or the good of the whole."[58]

The paradox of popular government is that in maintaining the
popular form, the causes of instability are in a sense protected.
One cannot prevent individuals from being judges in their own
cause without removing the legislative power from them. When this
happens, the government is either no longer popular, or no longer
wholly popular. And in protecting the diverse faculties of man, the
government thereby protects the latent cause of faction.

This led Publius to infer "that the *causes* of faction cannot be
removed, and that relief is only to be sought in the means of controlling its effects."[59] There is no other way in light of the para-
doxical situation.

The means by which Publius purported to secure stability while
attaining the public good is simply a reapplication, refinement, and
enlargement of Hobbes's means. Publius declared that "To secure
the public good and private rights against the danger of . . . faction,
and at the same time to preserve the spirit and the form of popular
government, is then the great object to which our inquiries are
directed."[60] The greatest threat to the public good and the private
rights of citizens stems from a majority faction. If the faction
amounts to less than a majority, its "sinister views" are defeated
by the republican principle, regular vote.[61] But when a faction consists of a majority of the people, "the form of popular government,
on the other hand, enables it to sacrifice to its ruling passion or
interest, both the public good and the rights of other citizens."[62]

A minority faction may "clog the administration" and "convulse
the society," but "it will be unable to execute and mask its violence
under the forms of the Constitution."[63] The great threat stems
from the majority that can execute violence under the mask of constitutional legitimacy through regular vote.[64]

Since the majority is "derived from the great body of the society,
not from an inconsiderable proportion, or a favored class of it,"[65]

"*The* problem for the friend of popular government is how to avoid the 'domestic convulsion' which results when the rich and the poor, the few and the many, as is their wont, are at each others' throats. Always before in popular governments the many, armed with political power, precipitated such convulsions."[66] Historically, democracies had witnessed attempts by the many to use government to take wealth away from the few. The few responded with mercenaries, and war was the result.

Two ways of preventing this confrontation are at the same time consistent with the spirit and form of republican government and the public good. The first is by preventing the simultaneous existence of the same passion or interest in a majority. The second is (given a failure to prevent a coexisting passion) by rendering the majority incapable of consenting and carrying into effect their "schemes of oppression."[67]

We shall first direct our attention to the second means, for it reinforces the first. We turn, therefore, to the principle of enlargement of the orbit. Publius introduced it first by observing that a "pure democracy" could not be extended over a large area since in that form "the citizens . . . assemble and administer the government in person."[68] To administer the government the citizens *have* to assemble. Given the means of transportation and communication of that time, the area over which a pure democracy could extend itself was limited to a few miles. As the form of pure democracy prevented its extension over a large area, it also ruled out the possibility of democracy as a cure for the "disease" of faction.[69] Its very nature required that the majority, in fact all, concert and communicate. Any time a common passion existed it would be felt by all, would be communicated to all, and their schemes would be carried into effect. Common passions and common interests also would be more likely under pure democracy. Within a limited area there are fewer interests, if for no other reason than the natural resources of that area.

The "true distinction" between democracy and a representative democracy is that the republican principle gives rise to a further difference on the basis of the size of the country and the number of citizens over which a democratic-republic can be extended.[70] Thus whereas enlargement of the orbit is severely restricted in a pure democracy, it is possible in a democratic republic.

An impure democracy is vastly superior to a pure democracy because it provides greater protection from a majority faction. The representative principle allows a larger country with more citizens because the people no longer have to assemble and administer the government in person. The practical problems of transportation and communication make it almost impossible for a majority faction to coalesce and further difficult to concert for action.[71]

This is but one of two beneficial effects of representative democracy. Enlargement of the orbit is of itself the second means of frustrating the pernicious effects of majority faction. It is beneficial in that it helps to make possible the conditions necessary for the prevention of a coexisting passion or interest within a majority faction. A greater number of citizens and size of territory is the "circumstance [which] principally . . . renders factious combinations less to be dreaded,"[72] in a representative democracy. "The smaller the society, the fewer probably will be the distinct parties and interests composing it; the fewer the distinct parties and interests, the more frequently will a majority be found of the same party. . . . Extend the sphere and you take in a greater variety of parties and interests; you make it less probable that a majority of the whole will have a common motive to invade the rights of other citizens."[73]

This, perhaps, is the most important statement in *The Federalist*. A majority faction is less likely to form when the sphere is extended, thereby taking in a greater variety of parties and interests. Should religion be the interest, the sects of Massachusetts will be counterbalanced by those of Rhode Island or Pennsylvania. Should the most common and durable source of faction, property, be the interest, the varieties of each kind of property are brought into play.

The problem of majority faction stemming from property had been that when the many came to perceive themselves as poor, they had an interest in common. This was directed against those who were not poor, who by their very condition were perceived by the many as the cause of their poverty, and were, therefore, regarded as an opposing rich class.[74] Thus the struggle that resulted in the dissolution of democracies in the past was caused by divisions over degree or amount of property.

The solution lay in changing the nature of the struggle from a class basis, centered on degree or amount of property, to a nonclass basis, centered on variety or kind of property. The greater number of kinds of property that could be brought into play would cause a greater amount of interests to be involved. Publius intended to change the confrontation from the basis rich versus poor to the basis of some of the rich and some of the poor versus some others of both classes, et cetera. As the number of alignments on this basis became greater, alignments along class lines became less likely. In other words, the solution lay in multiplying the number of interests within society.[75]

This attacks another "conventional" notion of that time. Democracy was believed best operable within a small area, but this was primarily applicable to a pure democracy. Democracy was also held to be more attuned to the virtues of an agrarian society. Men of the time needed only to appeal to the authority of the oracle, Montesquieu.

An agrarian society is limited to a smaller number of interests than a commercial society. With Publius, it was a matter of the more the merrier. As more and more kinds of interests develop, there is less and less chance of a struggle upon class lines. And the less likely are the chances of a struggle developing upon class lines, the less likely are the chances of majority faction developing. "Publius sees in the large commercial republic the possibility for the first time of subordinating the difference over amount of property to the difference over kind of property." [76]

Publius calls not simply for a multiplication of interests by bringing in a greater number through enlargement of the orbit. He calls for a proliferation of interests on the basis of future developments

will be derived from and dependent on the society, the society itself will be broken into so many parts, interests and classes of citizens, that the rights of individuals, or of the minority, will be in little danger from interested combinations of the majority. In a free government the security for civil rights must be the same as that for religious rights. It consists in the one case in the multiplicity of interests, and in the other in the multiplicity of sects." [84]

Within Congress that multiplicity was represented with all its ramifications. Interest would check interest, thereby checking the majority faction. Should a majority faction overcome the represented interests, the further check of separation of powers would tend to frustrate it.

The mechanical contrivance of separation of powers seems as if it would work in theory. But what of practice, especially in light of Publius's lack of faith in the written words of constitutional provisions? The constitution could give the executive and the judiciary the means "to stave off oppressive legislation; the veto, the president's legislative initiative, his discretion in the enforcement of the laws, judicial review." [85] Parchment means were not enough. "The great security against a gradual concentration of the several powers in the same department, consists in giving to those who administer each department the necessary constitutional means and personal motives to resist encroachments of the others. . . . Ambition must be made to counteract ambition. The interest of the man must be connected with the constitutional rights of the place." [86]

Separation of powers is a viable force against tyranny because of the same principle Publius applied to society. Because of their ambition and interest and because of their passion and interest, the executive and judiciary resist tyranny, thereby attaining an aspect of the public good. This represents a further attempt to attain the public good through the pursuit of private interest. Publius could say that the "policy of supplying, by opposite and rival interests, the defect of better motives, might be traced through the whole system of human affairs, private as well as public," [87] because he did his utmost to make it so.

The departments were constructed to make them as dissimilar as possible. Representatives were chosen by direct election for shorter periods; the President was chosen by indirect election for a longer term; judges were appointed for life, barring bad behavior. The very nature of executive and judicial powers differed from those of the legislative body. Even the legislative branch was divided into different branches "to render them, by different modes of election and different principles of action, as little connected with each other as the nature of their common functions and their common dependence on the society will admit."[88]

With the legislative, executive, and judicial branches being dissimilar, and with members of each led by their ambition to resist one another, "Why will they collaborate with the legislature in good actions, without which collaboration government would be reduced to the imbecility Publius despised, and collide with the legislature in its bad actions?"[89] This raises another question: why will the legislature ever initiate good actions?

Good legislative action is possible because majorities can form along good lines. Majorities also can be united by reason. "A coalition of a majority of the whole society could seldom take place on any other principles than those of justice and the general good," given "the great variety of interests, parties, and sects which it embraces." The passions tend to exert centrifugal force upon majorities, while reason exerts centripetal force.

Separation of powers cannot prevent a determined majority from having its way, but it functions as a retarder. The assumption underlying the principle is that a majority faction, based upon passion, is a short-lived entity. Time, then, can give men the opportunity for cool, sedate reflection, time for the passions to cool and give way to reason. For "Americans . . . seldom adopt and steadily persevere for many years in an erroneous opinion respecting their interests."[90] There are also times when man's private interest does not clash with the public good. Publius summed up his statements about man thus: "As there is a degree of depravity in mankind which requires a certain degree of circumspection and distrust, so there are other qualities in human nature which justify a certain portion of esteem and confidence. Republican government presupposes the existence of these qualities in a higher degree than any other form."[91] These qualities are of both reason and passion, and both can initiate good activities.

The ability of men in government to cooperate is based in part upon their ability, given time, to come to the good. But this ability is based primarily upon passion. "The desire of reward is one of the strongest incentives of human conduct . . . [and] the best security for the fidelity of mankind is to make their interest coincide with their duty. . . . Even the love of fame, the ruling passion of the noblest minds . . . prompt[s] a man to plan and undertake extensive and arduous enterprises for the public benefit."[92]

One of Publius's better students, and perhaps one of Hobbes's as well, saw the deeper significance of this principle. Hobbes has been condemned not only as antilibertarian, but also as atheistic. Many believe that, for Hobbes, religion and God were really things to be used; that is, they were good insofar as they were useful. This completely misses Hobbes's point. Hobbes said that the moral influence religion exerts upon men decreases as religion becomes less influential upon them. When this happens, one thing only will oblige men—fear. There is one who is not obliged by fear—the sovereign monarch. He must be brought into line with the public good by identifying his private interest with that good.

The following statement by de Tocqueville shows at once both the problem Hobbes contended with and the superiority of Publius's solution over that of Hobbes. "Do you not see that religious belief is shaken, and the divine notion of right is declining?—that morality is debased, and the notion of moral right is therefore fading away? Argument is substituted for faith, and calculation for the impulses of sentiment. If, in the midst of this general disruption, you do not succeed in connecting the notion of right with that of private interest, which is the only immutable point in the human heart, what means will you have of governing the world except by fear?"[93] The notion of right must be connected with private interest. Hobbes favored such a connection with the sovereign, but not with the subjects. He therefore needed a common power to hold them in awe or fear. Publius, on the other hand, connected private interest with right throughout "the whole system of human affairs," including the sovereign people *and* their government. Through his more extensive and refined means of using private interest to attain the public good, Publius limited the need for and use of fear as a means of governing to as great an extent as it ever will or can be restricted, barring a change in human nature. As Publius noted, "I am clearly of opinion it is your interest to adopt it. I am convinced that this is the safest course for your liberty, your dignity, and your happiness." [94]

FIVE CONCLUSIONS NOW HAVE BEEN DRAWN: (1) Hobbes's political theory is in harmony with that of the Declaration of Independence; (2) Locke's solution to the problem of societal instability is inadequate; (3) the Founding Fathers rejected Locke's solution; (4) they adopted not only a Hobbesian definition of the problem but a Hobbesian solution as well; and (5) they did this while establishing a profoundly democratic society.

Insofar as we may be termed a Lockean or Hobbesian nation, we are certainly more Hobbesian than Lockean. Our political system is not characterized by unchecked majority rule—that is, checked if at all by Locke's "will independent of society," by the prerogative of the monarch. Nor are the ends of our society restricted to the protection of life, liberty, and estate. Locke's "property" is too narrow a category, being only a part of a larger, more inclusive end, happiness.

Happiness, on the other hand, is *the* end of Hobbes's thought. A substantial implementation of that thought is found throughout our political system, our basic political documents, and our political ideas. At the same time, Hobbes's belief that monarchy was the only form of government capable of securing both the rights of man and societal stability is not an American political idea. The *reason* he supported monarchy, albeit borrowed, refined, and enlarged, however, is indeed an American political idea.

Additionally, as the founder of modern political theory, or at least of libertarian theory, Hobbes made a significant contribution, not to just our American form of government but to all popular government. Few can deny the significance of his passionate-natured man, of his making all men equal in rights, and of his notion of an essential equality of ability, the prerequisite justification of modern democratic-libertarian theory. It would be a mistake, however, to close our eyes to the shortcomings of his system. As with Locke's, that system fell short of securing liberty and, ultimately, stability.

All of what has gone before seems to come to this: if we can say our political thought and system reflect the teaching of any one theorist, that theorist is Publius. Martin Diamond, who understood that teaching as well as any, was reluctant to call it great political theory. I have no such reluctance.

Publius's system accomplishes two things: it shows the way to secure the rights of man while providing stability. In that it provides us with the means to protect the lives of men and bless them with happiness, subject primarily to individual liabilities, it provides the means for attaining the right ordering of society and man's right life. Publius's theory is theory *par excellence*, such superior theory that it has needed little modification. And this raises a question that I believe deserves mention in closing.

Many apologists for American political theory seem to have taken Tocqueville at his word that a democratic society creates a certain "addiction to practical rather than theoretical science." This was seen as one of the results of equality, a desire in man to judge everything for himself. Rather, I believe the answer lies in the obvious, but little-mentioned fact that such "theoretical" science is not needed here. Theory usually arises when men criticize existing political systems. We may view the entire history of natural law or natural right as a complex of normative symbols existing above the political situation and used as bases for criticism. When the existing situation is perceived as not in need of such criticism, theory does not develop. I suspect the reason so little theory has evolved in the United States is that, for the most part, the *grand* issues have been resolved, which has left us free to concentrate upon those "practical" sciences.

NOTES

PREFACE

1. Under the pseudonym Publius, John Jay, James Madison, and Alexander Hamilton published a series of eighty-five essays in New York newspapers. The combined papers—Jay wrote five, Madison twenty-six, Hamilton fifty-one, and three are of unknown authorship—were called *The Federalist*. A defense of the new constitution and a plea for the republican form of government, *The Federalist* is a classic document on constitutional theory.

CHAPTER 1. *The Nature of the American Political Heritage*

1. See Louis Hartz, *The Liberal Tradition in America* (New York: Harcourt, Brace and Co., 1955), pp. 4–13, 17–18, 26, 59–63.
2. Jefferson to Henry Lee, 8 May 1825, *The Writings of Thomas Jefferson*, ed. Andrew A. Lipscomb, 20 vols. (Washington, D.C.: The Thomas Jefferson Memorial Association, 1905), XVI, 117. See also I, 17–39; IV, 34; and XV, 462–64.
3. In an unpublished annotated bibliography of The American Statesman's Library, Douglass Adair noted that Jefferson owned copies of *De Cive* and the *Translation of Thucydides*, and Madison owned a copy of *Leviathan*. It is interesting that only Locke's *Second Treatise* is included in this library, compared with the whole of Hobbes's works.
4. For a discussion of the insufficiencies of the most widely read commentary supporting the sole preservation of life thesis,

see George Mace, "An Abuse of Words," *Western Political Quarterly*, 20, No. 3 (1967), 639−44.
5. See Hartz, pp. 79−81. See also Richard Hofstadter, *The American Political Tradition* (New York: Vintage, 1969), pp. 3, 5, 16. Hereafter cited as Hofstadter.
6. Vernon L. Parrington, *Main Currents in American Thought*, I (New York: Harcourt, Brace and Co., 1927), especially 279−91; Charles A. Beard, *An Economic Interpretation of the Constitution* (New York: Macmillan Co., 1913), passim; Samuel Eliot Morison and Henry Steele Commager, *The Growth of the American Republic*, I (London: Oxford University Press, 1956), pp. 277−78; and Hofstadter, pp. 3−18, 354−55.
7. George Mace, "The Antidemocratic Character of Judicial Review," 60 *Cal. L. Rev.* 1148 (1972). (Idea expressed herein by permission of publisher.)

CHAPTER 2. *Locke's Political Theory Revisited*

1. John Locke, *Two Treatises of Government*, ed. Peter Laslett (Cambridge: Cambridge University Press, 1960), p. 298, sec. 19. All references to Locke's work by section will be to the *Second Treatise*.
2. Sec. 6, and, especially, sec. 19. Cf. sec. 181.
3. Sec. 168. See also secs. 87−94.
4. Sec. 21. See also sec. 176.
5. Sec. 95. See also sec. 54, sec. 123.
6. Sec. 132. (Italics mine).
7. See *The Oxford History of the American People* (New York: Oxford University Press, 1965), p. 95; and Philip Abrams, *John Locke: Two Tracts on Government* (Cambridge: Cambridge University Press, 1967), passim.
8. C. B. MacPherson, "Natural Rights in Hobbes and Locke," in *Political Theory and the Rights of Man*, ed. D. D. Raphael

(Bloomington: Indiana University Press, 1967), p. 2. Hereafter cited as MacPherson.

9. Ibid., p. 1.
10. Ibid., especially pp. 1, 2, 8.
11. Sec. 54. See also sec. 181.
12. Sec. 50. See also chap. V.
13. "Happiness" appears three times: (1) in reference to what is meant by children honoring their parents, p. 329 (sec. 66); (2) in reference to the inability of absolute monarchy to attain it, p. 345 (sec. 92); (3) in reference to monarchies' ability to attain it in the early stages or beginnings of civil society, p. 356 (sec. 107). "Happy" appears once in a quotation from Hooker, where Hooker suggests men enter civil society to procure "Peace, Tranquility, and happy Estate," p. 345n. (sec. 91). The closest that Locke comes to happiness as a statement of his own position is found in his references to the end of civil society. He refers infrequently to the "comfort" of the people. Compare his statements concerning the ends of government: pp. 304, 316, 325, 329–30, 336, 346–47, 349, 352, 356, 360, 368, 371, 373, 377, 379, 385, 388, 389, 399, 425, 428, 430, 433–34, and 442 (secs. 26, 42, 57, 66, 76, 92–95, 101, 107, 110–11, 123, 130, 134, 136–37, 139, 149, 155–56, 171, 211, 217, 222, 226–27, and 239).
14. This inconsistency is probably due to the fact, as Peter Laslett demonstrated, that various parts of the *Second Treatise* were written at widely separated points in time. It appears that the extended notion of property was superimposed upon previously written sections containing the restricted notion. See Laslett, pp. 30–36 and 45–65. Locke's "property" falls into three categories of meaning: (1) a restricted meaning of material possessions: pp. 286, 289, 304, 307–8, 310, 313–14, 316–18, 320, 329, 332, 334–35, 355, 364, 366, 371, 378, 381, 385, 412–13, 417, and 433–34 (secs. 3, 6, 25, 28, 30–32, 35–36, 38–40, 44–46, 50–51, 65, 69, 74–75, 105, 116, 120, 131, 138, 142, 149, 192–94, 200, and 226–28), (2) an extended meaning of life and

estate, liberty and estate, or life, liberty and estate: pp. 305, 324–25, 341–42, 347, 349, 375–77, 380, 399, 401, 414, 417–18, 430, and 433–36 (secs. 27, 57, 59, 85, 87–88, 94–95, 135–37, 140, 171, 173, 196, 199, 201, 222, 226, 228–29, 231, and 239), and (3) instances where it is not clear which meaning, restricted or extended, is intended: pp. 339, 345, 368–70, 379, and 402 (secs. 82, 91, 123–24, 127, 139, and 174). Compare with Laslett's listings: pp. 341n. and 518.

15. Abrams, *Two Tracts.*

CHAPTER 3. *Hobbes: The Basis of American Natural Rights Heritage*

1. To facilitate reference to Hobbes's works from sources other than mine, citations will also be made to the work by chapter and section, which will follow in parentheses. Thomas Hobbes, *Leviathan*, ed. A. R. Waller (Cambridge: Cambridge University Press, 1904), p. 81 (pt. I, chap. XIII). Hereafter cited as Waller. References to Hobbes's other works will be from *The English Works of Thomas Hobbes*, ed. William Molesworth, 11 vols. (London: John Bohn, 1839–1840. Hereafter cited as *E. W.* For other statements on the equality of men, see *E. W.*, II, 6–7 (*De Cive*, chap. I, art. iii); IV, 81–82, 84, 102–3, (*De Corpore Politico*, pt. I, chap. I, arts. i, ii, x; chap. IV, art. i).

2. Waller, p. 152 (pt. II, chap. XXI). See also *E. W.*, II, 9–11.

3. Ibid., pp. 129–32 (pt. II, chap. XIX).

4. For an interesting essay on some of the other contrasts that can be drawn, see Sterling P. Lamprecht, "Hobbes and Hobbism," *The American Political Science Review*, 34, no. 1 (1940), pp. 31–53. See also Thomas Hobbes, *De Cive or the Citizen*, ed. and intro. by Sterling P. Lamprecht (New York: Appleton-Century-Crofts, Inc., 1949), pp. xx–xxx.

5. Waller, p. 84. See also *E. W.*, II, 11 (*De Cive*, chap. I, sec. 12).
6. Ibid., p. 83. See also *E. W.*, II, 11 (*De Cive*, chap. I, sec. 12).
7. J. Roland Pennock, "Hobbes's Confusing 'Clarity'—The Case of Liberty," *The American Political Science Review*, 54, no. 2 (1960), 428.
8. See Waller, p. xiii (Dedication).
9. Ibid., pp. 139–40.
10. Ibid., p. 89.
11. Ibid., p. 242 (pt. II, chap. xxx). See also *E. W.*, II, 166–68 (*De Cive*, chap. XIII, secs. 1–4).
12. See ibid., p. 108 (pt. I, chap. XV); and *E. W.*, II, 45–46 (*De Cive*, chap. III, sec. 27), IV, 107–8, 114–16 (*De Corpore Politico*, pt. I, chap. IV, sec. 10, chap. V, secs. 8–12, especially sec. 10).
13. Ibid., p. xviii.
14. Ibid., pp. 267–68 (pt. II, chap. XXI).
15. Ibid., p. xiv.
16. Ibid., pp. 525–26.
17. Ibid., p. 156 (pt. II, chap. XXI).
18. Ibid., p. 152.
19. Ibid., p. 154.
20. Ibid., pp. 243–44 (pt. II, chap. XXX).
21. Ibid., p. 244. See also p. 506 (pt. IV, chap. XXXXVI).
22. Ibid., p. 89 (pt. I, chap. XIV). See also Ibid., p. 105; and *E. W.*, II, 39 (*De Cive*, chap. III, sec. 14), IV, 103 (*De Corpore Politico*, pt. I, chap. IV, sec. 2). It also should be noted that it was Hobbes, not Locke, who wrote explicitly of inalienable rights.
23. Ibid., p. 89.
24. MacPherson, n. 44.
25. Waller, pp. 242–43 (pt. 11, chap. XXX).
26. See ibid., pp. 31–33 and 81–86 (esp. p. 84) (pt. I, chaps. VI and XIII). The major theme of chapter XIII, entitled "*Of the* NATURALL CONDITION *of Mankind, as concerning their Felicity, and Misery*," is that the natural state is a

dreadful one, devoid of felicity and high on misery, and that the reason men leave that state is for the express purposes of peace and commodious living.

27. E. W., II, 167 (*De Cive*, chap. XIII, sec. 4). See also E. W., IV, 85, 162, 214 (*De Corpore Politico*, pt. I, chap. I, sec. 12, pt. II, chap. V, sec. 1, chap. IX, sec. 2).

CHAPTER 4. *On the Nature and Condition of Man*

1. Waller, p. xx (*Leviathan*, Intro.).
2. Ibid.
3. Leo Strauss, *The Political Philosophy of Hobbes*, American ed. (Chicago: University of Chicago Press, 1952), p. 1.
4. Leo Strauss, *Thoughts on Machiavelli* (Glencoe, Ill.: The Free Press, 1958), p. xx.
5. Ibid., p. 280.
6. Ibid., p. 281.
7. Ibid.
8. Ibid.
9. Ibid., p. 280.
10. Ibid.
11. Ibid.
12. Ibid., p. 282.
13. Waller, p. 81 (*Leviathan*, pt. I, chap. XIII).
14. Ibid., pp. 82–83.
15. Ibid., p. 63 (chap. XI).
16. Ibid., p. 54 (chap. X).
17. Ibid., p. 63.
18. Ibid.
19. Ibid., p. 83.
20. Ibid., p. 33 (chap. VI). See also p. 34 for the definition of "vain-glory."
21. Ibid., p. 83.
22. Ibid., p. 54.
23. Ibid., p. 83.
24. Ibid., p. 84.
25. Ibid., p. 83.
26. Ibid.
27. Ibid.
28. Ibid., p. 84.
29. Ibid., pp. 85–86.
30. Ibid. In his excellent book, *The Political Theory of Possessive Individualism* (Oxford: Clarendon Press, 1962), C. B. MacPherson emphasized the implications "competition" held for man in Hobbes's state of nature. For MacPherson, competi-

tion is *the* explanation for the ill condition. Although Mac-Pherson and I are in essential agreement on the causes of the ill condition, we disagree sharply on the notions of the state of nature, man's *nature*, political obligation, and Hobbes's ultimate aims. Further, where I am more concerned with the political aspects of Hobbes's thought, MacPherson is more concerned with economic aspects. See pp. 9–100.

31. Waller, pp. 85–86.
32. Ibid., p. 86.
33. Ibid.
34. Ibid., p. 109 (chap. XV). In this statement, "law . . . is the word of him, *that by right* hath command over others . . . ," we find the means of determining whether there is any other norm in Hobbes's society besides power. "Right" determines what sort of justification Hobbes sees necessary for the exercise of rule.
35. Ibid., p. 8 (chap. III).
36. Hobbes used "thought" and "imagination" interchangeably.
37. Ibid., p. 9.
38. Ibid.
39. Ibid.
40. Ibid., pp. 9–10.
41. Ibid., p. 10.
42. Ibid., pp. 10–11.
43. Ibid., p. 11.
44. Ibid., pp. 11–12.
45. Ibid. These predictions are also called "Foresight" and "Wisdom" but they are nothing more than guesses. See Waller, p. 11.
46. Hobbes also discussed the distinctive feature of man, which is not "prudence," but "understanding." See Waller, pp. 13–21 (chap. IV), especially p. 20.
47. Ibid., pp. 12–21.
48. Ibid., p. 21.
49. Ibid., p. 22 (chap. V).
50. Ibid., p. 26.
51. Ibid., p. 25.
52. Ibid., p. 109 (chap. XV).
53. Ibid., p. 87 (chap. XIV).
54. Ibid., p. 86.
55. Ibid., p. 87.
56. Ibid., p. 86.
57. Ibid., p. 87.
58. Ibid., pp. 86–87.
59. Ibid., p. 86.
60. Ibid.

61. Ibid., p. 87.
62. Ibid.
63. Ibid.
64. Ibid.
65. Ibid.
66. Ibid.
67. Ibid., pp. 87–88.
68. Ibid., p. 88.
69. Ibid.
70. Ibid.
71. See Joseph Tussman, *Obligation and the Body Politic* (New York: Oxford University Press, 1960).
72. Waller, pp. 88–89.
73. Ibid.
74. Ibid., pp. 242–43 (chap. XXX).
75. *E. W.*, II, 167 (*De Cive*, chap. XIII, sec. 4). See also *E. W.*, IV, 85, 162, 214 (*De Corpore Politico*, pt. I, chap. I, sec. 12, pt. II, chap. V, sec. 1, chap. IX, sec. 2).
76. Ibid., p. 169 (*De Cive*, chap. XIII, sec. 6).
77. Waller, p. 118 (chap. XVII).
78. Ibid., p. 119.
79. Ibid., p. 117.
80. Ibid., p. 118.
81. Ibid., pp. 118–19.
82. Ibid., p. 119.
83. Ibid.

CHAPTER 5. *Hobbes's Speciousness*

1. J. Roland Pennock, "Hobbes's Confusing 'Clarity'—The Case of Liberty," *The American Political Science Review*, 54, No. 2 (1960), 428. Hereafter cited as Pennock.
2. I am indebted to C. B. MacPherson for indicating the significance of this point. See *The Political Theory of Possessive Individualism* (Oxford: Clarendon Press, 1962), p. 20.
3. Waller, p. 523 (Review and Conclusion). See also p. 522. As we shall see, Hobbes delivered a beforehand answer to Hume's attack on social contract theory.
4. Ibid., p. 428.
5. Ibid., p. 429.
6. Waller, pp. 35–36 (chap. VI), and compare chap. I, above,

chaps. VI and VII of *Leviathan* with Pennock, pp. 429–30, especially n. 10.

7. Pennock, pp. 428–30.

8. Ibid., p. 429.

9. Wit is an aspect of ability.

10. Waller, p. 86.

11. Ibid., p. 147 (chap. XXI).

12. Ibid., p. 36 (chap. VI).

13. Pennock, p. 429, n. 10.

14. Waller, p. 36 (chap. VI).

15. Ibid., p. 35.

16. See Pennock, p. 429, n. 10, and compare with Waller, p. 36.

17. Waller, p. 148 (chap. XXI).

18. Ibid.

19. Ibid., pp. 36, 148.

20. Ibid.

21. Pennock, p. 429.

22. Ibid., p. 436.

23. Ibid., p. 429.

24. Waller, p. 148.

25. Ibid.

26. Ibid.

27. Ibid.

28. Ibid., p. 32 (chap. VI).

29. See Waller, pp. 31–32.

30. Pennock, p. 430.

31. Ibid.

32. Ibid.

33. See Waller, pp. 147–49 (chap. XXI).

34. Compare with Hobbes's argument that men give up some of their liberty to preserve other rights.

35. See Thomas Hobbes, *Leviathan*, ed. Michael Oakeshott (Oxford: Basil Blackwell, 1955), p. 138; or Waller, p. 149 (chap. XXI).

36. Pennock, p. 430, See also notes 28 and 29 above.

37. Waller, p. 149.

38. Pennock, p. 430.

39. Waller, p. 149.

40. Ibid., pp. 149–50. It is interesting to note that Pennock builds a "paradox" on the basis of the last sentence of this quotation. Apparently he is not sure whether we ought to concern ourselves with this material or not. See n. 36 above; and Pennock, p. 430, n. 13.

41. Ibid., p. 155.

42. See n. 35 above.

43. Waller, p. 149.

44. Ibid., p. 152.

45. For Pennock this is and is not a paradox. It is a paradox, but

on the other hand it is resolved by Hobbes. See Pennock, p. 430.

46. Waller, p. 152.
47. Ibid.
48. Ibid., pp. 152–53.
49. Pennock, p. 429.
50. Waller, p. 153.
51. Ibid.

52. Ibid., p. 94 (chap. XIV).
53. Ibid., p. 139 (chap. XX).
54. Ibid.
55. Ibid.
56. Ibid.
57. Ibid.

58. Ibid., p. 140 (chap. XX).
59. Ibid., p. 522 (Review and Conclusion).
60. Ibid., p. 142.
61. Ibid.
62. Ibid., p. 522 (Review and Conclusion). Also see p. 65 (chap. XI).
63. MacPherson, "Natural Rights in Hobbes and Locke," p. 20.
64. Waller, pp. 525–26.
65. Ibid., p. 89.
66. Ibid., p. 88.

CHAPTER 6. *Hobbes's "Absolute" Power*

1. Waller, p. 118 (chap. XVII).
2. Ibid., p. 131 (chap. XIX).
3. Ibid., p. 427 (chap. XXXXII); *E. W.*, II, 83, 166 (*De Cive*, chap. VI, sec. 14, chap. XIII, sec. 2); IV, 206, 213 (*De Corpore Politico*, pt. II, chap. VIII, sec. 6, chap. IX, sec. 1).
4. Waller, p. 232 (chap. XXIX).
5. Ibid., p. 46 (chap. VIII).
6. Ibid., p. 115. Hobbes used "terrour" synonymously with "feare." See pp. 32–33 (chap. VI).
7. Ibid., p. 232.
8. (New York and Burlingame: Harcourt, Brace & World, Inc.,

1962), p. 116. See also the revised version of this book by the same author in *Western Political Theory: from Its Origin to the Present* (New York: Harcourt, Brace & World, Inc., 1968), p. 329.

9. Waller, p. 128 (chap. XVIII).

10. E. W., II, 70 (*De Cive*, chap. V, sec. 11).

11. Waller, pp. 146, 406 (chaps. XX, XXXXII).

12. Ibid., p. 93.

13. E. W., II, 88 (*De Cive*, chap. VI, sec. 18).

14. Waller, p. 128 (chap. XVIII). See also p. 119 (chap. XVII).

15. Ibid., p. 159 (chap. XXII). See also Waller, p. 130 (chap. XIX), E. W., II, 88 (*De Cive*, chap. VI, secs. 17, 18).

16. E. W., II, 96n. (*De Cive*, chap. VII, sec. 4, n.).

17. Ibid.

18. Ibid.

19. Waller, p. 236 (chap. XXIX); E. W., IV, 38, 135 (*De homine*, chap. VIII, sec. 4; *De Corpore Politico*, pt. II, chap. I, sec. 16).

20. Ibid. However, Hobbes did say that one of the advantages of a monarchy over a democracy was a monarch could not disagree with himself out of "envy or interest," as could happen in an assembly. He saw envy and interest, moreover, as causes of civil war. I believe, due to his choice of words, that this is little more than a make-weight argument. Hobbes never said the disagreement would occur; it may occur since it is theoretically possible. See Waller, p. 132 (chap. XIX).

21. Waller, p. 126 (chap. XVIII).

22. Ibid., pp. 126–27. See also p. 236 (chap. XXXI); E. W., IV, 134–35 (*De Corpore Politico*, pt. I, chap. I, secs. 15, 16, 17).

Hobbes would term as faction the divisions of citizens supporting the unestablished sovereign. The definition he gave to factions within an assembly is "a number of men . . . without Authority, consult a part, to contrive the guidance of the rest . . . as being a fradulent seducing of the Assembly for their particular interest." *E. W.*, IV, 168–69 (*De Corpore Politico*, pt. II, chap. V, sec. 8).

23. Ibid., pp. 239–40.
24. Ibid., p. xiv (Dedication).
25. Ibid., p. 126 (chap. XVIII). For Hobbes there were but three forms of government: monarchy, aristocracy, and democracy. The sovereign power was placed in the hands of one man, an assembly representing a part of the commonwealth, or an assembly representing all. The latter was a democracy or "Popular Common-wealth." See Waller, p. 129 (chap. XIX). See also p. 135 (chap. XIX).
26. Ibid., p. 129 (chap. XIX).
27. Ibid., pp. 34, 46, 130, 406 (chaps. XIX, XX, XXXXII).
28. *E. W.*, II, 166 (*De Cive*, chap. XIII, sec. 1).
29. For example, see Waller, p. 134 (chap. XIX).
30. Ibid., p. 130.
31. See Waller, p. 132 (chap. XVIII), and passim.
32. Ibid.
33. Ibid.
34. Ibid., see p. 131.
35. Ibid.
36. Ibid.
37. Ibid.
38. Ibid.
39. Ibid.
40. Ibid.
41. Ibid., p. 32 (chap. VI).
42. Ibid.
43. Ibid., p. 55 (chap. X).
44. For a definition of "Joy," see Waller, p. 31.
45. Ibid., p. 29 (chap. VI).
46. Ibid., p. 38 (chap. VII).
47. Ibid., p. 64 (chap. XI).
48. Ibid.
49. Ibid.

CHAPTER 7. *The Federalist: From the Truth of Speculation to the Utility of Practice*

1. Waller, p. xiii (Dedication).
2. Ibid., p. 268 (chap. XXXI).

3. Martin Diamond, "The Federalist," in Leo Strauss et al., *History of Political Philosophy* (Chicago: Rand McNally & Co., 1963), p. 573. Hereafter cited as Diamond.

4. Ibid. 6. Ibid.

5. Ibid., p. 574. 7. Ibid.

8. Alexander Hamilton et al., *The Federalist*, intro. by E. M. Earle (New York: The Modern Library, n.d.), no. 51, p. 337. Hereafter cited as *The Federalist*. See also no. 15, p. 92. "Why has government been instituted at all? Because the passions of men will not conform to the dictates of reason and justice, without constraint."

9. Ibid., no. 6, p. 27. 11. Ibid., no. 15, p. 86.

10. Ibid., no. 1, pp. 4–5. 12. Ibid., no. 75, p. 487.

13. For references to some of the passions, see Meynard Smith, "Reason, Passion, and Political Freedom in the *Federalist*," *The Journal of Politics*, 22, no. 3 (1960), 525, n. 10; James P. Acaulan, "The Federalist and Human Nature," *The Review of Politics*, 21 (October, 1959), 662–63; Benjamin F. Wright, "The Federalist on the Nature of Political Man," *Ethics*, 2 (January, 1949), passim.

14. Waller, p. 53 (pt. I, chap. IX). See also pp. 108–09 (pt. I, chap. XV).

15. Ibid., p. 147 (pt. II, chap. XXI).

16. *The Federalist*, no. 9, p. 48.

17. Ibid. 19. Ibid., pp. 58–61.

18. Ibid., p. 49. 20. Ibid., no. 14, p. 80.

21. Ibid. See also Diamond, p. 581.

22. Ibid. 27. Ibid., p. 59.

23. Ibid. 28. Ibid., no. 14, p. 80.

24. Ibid., p. 81. 29. Diamond, pp. 579–81.

25. Diamond, p. 581. 30. *The Federalist*, no. 10, p. 53.

26. *The Federalist*, no. 10, p. 58. 31. Ibid.

32. Ibid., no. 10, pp. 57–58.

33. Diamond quoting Pierson, p. 580.

34. *The Federalist*, no. 10, pp. 53–54.

35. Ibid., p. 54.
36. Ibid.
37. Ibid.
38. Ibid., no. 28, p. 173.
39. Ibid., no. 10, p. 54. Compare with the above definition of faction given by Hobbes, see chap. VI, n. 22.
40. Ibid., pp. 54–55.
41. Ibid.
42. Ibid., p. 55.
43. Ibid.
44. Ibid.
45. Ibid.
46. Ibid.
47. Ibid., p. 56.
48. Ibid.
49. For Publius's use of history, see especially in *The Federalist*, no. 6.
50. Ibid., p. 56.
51. Ibid.
52. Ibid.
53. Ibid., p. 57.
54. Ibid., p. 56.
55. Ibid., pp. 56–57.
56. Ibid., p. 57.
57. Ibid.
58. Ibid.
59. Ibid.
60. Ibid., pp. 57–58.
61. Ibid., p. 57.
62. Ibid.
63. Ibid.
64. Ibid.
65. Ibid., no. 39, p. 244.
66. Diamond, p. 589.
67. *The Federalist*, p. 58.
68. Ibid.
69. Ibid.
70. Ibid., p. 59.
71. The representative principle also has an advantage inherently, and not due to an effect. The public views are refined and enlarged by being passed through a chosen body of citizens. See *The Federalist*, p. 59; and Diamond, p. 587.
72. Ibid., p. 60.
73. Ibid., pp. 60–61.
74. Diamond, p. 590. Note that this division is *likely* in a small republic. It is only *possible* in a large one if there are not many varied interests.
75. Ibid., pp. 590–92.
76. Ibid., p. 591.
77. Professor Douglass Adair attributed Publius's solution to the problem of majority faction to Hume. I believe that the

principles of enlargement of the orbit and refinement are most certainly taken from Hume. However, the notion of enlargement of orbit may be found in germ in chapter XXIV of *Leviathan*. The essential aspect of the solution is the development of varied interests which will check one another. I believe Professor Adair wrongly attributed this notion to Hume: Madison says, "The society becomes broken into a greater variety of interests . . . which check each other." Hume says, "The force of popular currents and tides is in a great measure, broken." These two statements are not the same. There is no mention of interest, varieties thereof, nor interests checking one another. Madison's indebtedness to Hume seems even more dubious in light of Hume's full statement. That which breaks (checks) the force of popular currents and tides is not interests checking one another. Rather, Hume believed that people dispersed in small bodies become "more susceptible both of reason and order." It is not passionate, self-seeking interests that check each other. Hume's solution is not the attainment of the public interest through the pursuit of private interest. The public interest is attained because geographic dispersion renders men more *reasonable*. See *The Huntington Library Quarterly*, "That Politics may be Reduced to a Science: David Hume, James Madison, the Tenth *Federalist*," 20, no. 1 (1961), especially pp. 351, 354, n. 10; and David Hume, *Essays, Moral, Political, and Literary* (London, 1758), I, 113.

78. *The Federalist*, no. 51, p. 337.
79. Ibid., no. 47, p. 313.   82. Ibid.
80. Ibid., no. 48, pp. 322–23.   83. Ibid.
81. Ibid., no. 51, p. 339.   84. Ibid., pp. 339–40.
85. Diamond, p. 586.
86. *The Federalist*, p. 337. See also Diamond, p. 586.
87. Ibid.
88. Ibid., p. 338.

89. Diamond, p. 586.
90. *The Federalist*, no. 3, p. 13.
91. Ibid., no. 55, p. 365.
92. Ibid., no. 72, p. 470. Compare with Publius's motives in no.
     1, p. 6.
93. Alexis de Tocqueville, *Democracy in America*, ed. Richard D.
     Heffner (New York: New American Library, 1956), p. 106.
94. *The Federalist*, no. 1, p. 6.

BIBLIOGRAPHICAL ESSAY

CHARLES A. BEARD's *An Economic Interpretation of the Constitution* (New York: The Macmillan Company, 1913) is probably the first effort at a systematic treatment in which the problem of the Founding Fathers is portrayed as that of careful adjustment and compromise of the interests of conflicting groups. It is, so he argues, economic forces that condition great movements in politics; and politics and constitutional law are but a reflex of the contending interests. In chapters six and seven, for example, Beard analyzes the Constitution and the expositions of it found in the *Federalist* to demonstrate that the chief constitutional concern was with economic problems and not with abstract conceptions of liberty and justice. Beard signally fails to prove, however, that the leaders in the movement for a stronger national government were influenced by their financial interests rather than by the public welfare. A defect, then, is that he does not undertake to test his "theory" by analyzing the votes taken in the convention on specific questions. All in all, the tendency of Beard's economic interpretation of history is to reduce everything to a sordid basis of personal interest. Beard's main deficiency is that he simply misses the major innovation of the American Founding Fathers, namely, the conversion of economic-social conflict from confrontation based on the amount of property to confrontation based on the kind of property.

The core of Louis Hartz's argument in *The Liberal Tradition in America* (New York: Harcourt, Brace and Company, 1955) is that the distinctive feature of American development has been the absence of a feudal stage; hence the American people never developed the extreme, bitter ideological differences that racked Europe and shaped its political history. Thus, the argument goes, American development has been unique from its very beginning, since the country was "born free." The only real political clash in America, then, has been between the big-propertied Whigs and the small-propertied Progressives, who, measured by a European yardstick, have had more common beliefs than differing ones. Hartz also argues that to the extent that we can find any major source of American constitutionalism, it is the "Lockian creed," which he sees "enshrined in the Constitution."

In *The American Political Tradition* (New York: Vintage Books, 1969) Richard Hofstadter's object was not to establish some single overarching theory about American political leadership, but rather to make a number of critical comments on certain political figures. He took—with modifications—a biographical approach. In this volume the reader finds careful scholarship and penetrating incisiveness. Hofstadter contended that concern for property rights, regard for individual opportunity, and enlightened self-interest as the motivation for social progress had been the core of American political belief until the advent of the New Deal. To be successful, Hofstadter suggested, politicians must be opportunistic and pragmatic, though they must not seem so, no inclusive and systematic conception of American politics can be put into practice. The competition of interests Madison and his colleagues recognized in 1787 and made the basis of the division of governmental powers goes on. It is not difficult to find in *The American Political Tradition* the theme that if Locke and Montesquieu inspired the Founding Fathers in 1776, by 1787 they perceived the world through the eyes of Hobbes.

Lee C. McDonald's scholarship, cogent reasoning, and hard analysis are notable in *Western Political Theory: From its Origin to the Present* (New York: Harcourt, Brace & World, Inc., 1968), an expansion of his own work first published in 1962 (chapters 10–28 are from the original). The book is further notable for additional material covering behavioral studies, logical positivism, and systems-analysis approaches. It also contains a good index and bibliography.

In dealing with his subjects, namely Hobbes, the Levellers, Harrington, and Locke, what ultimately interests C. B. MacPherson in *The Political Theory of Possessive Individualism* (Oxford: Clarendon Press, 1962) is the light shed by his theorists on the whole problem of political obligation. His purpose was to discover what kind of fundamental repair should be attempted to recover the desirable values of individualism while discarding its excesses. It is no accident, then, that the author takes a Marxist approach, though his Marxism is refreshingly undogmatic. His lengthy treatment on Hobbes is the best part of the book, though perhaps repetitious. Whereas Locke is seen as the most "bourgeois" of his thinkers, Hobbes appears as a distant ancestor of liberalism, as well as an important precursor of Bentham. Hobbes also is seen as the founder of modern political philosophy, the most formidable of English political theorists. The theses that Hobbes's state of nature was an abstraction of the "competitive-market" elements of the seventeenth century, and that Hobbes, "in building on the compulsions and morality of the market, penetrated to the heart of the problem of obligation in modern possessive societies" are most scholarly and elegantly argued.

In *Main Currents in American Thought,* I (New York: Harcourt, Brace and Company, 1927) Vernon L. Parrington shows how the ideas characteristic of the American people have flowered in most of the colonial literature. He presents a series of biographies exemplifying the advance of thought from generation to generation and gives not simply an aesthetic point of view, but also an account of the important economic, political, and social theories put forth in the works of American men of letters.

In *Thoughts on Machiavelli* (Glencoe, Ill.: The Free Press, 1959) Leo Strauss has omitted all references to the scholarly literature on Machiavelli of the past hundred years. His approach is not only at variance with modern scholarship but it is also based on certain abstract propositions and philosophical presuppositions. It also seems divorced from a historical context; Machiavelli is neither taken as a product of the intellectual peculiarities of the Italian

Renaissance, nor understood within the context of Florentine history. Rather, he is seen against a background of classical thought.

Strauss believed previous students have failed to read Machiavelli "in the right way" because they did not reach out to the "hidden meaning" that contains Machiavelli's "true opinion." And this true opinion can only be discovered by "carefully reading between the lines." One cannot understand Machiavelli's works unless one "ponders over them day and night." Strauss argues that Machiavelli actually concealed the revolutionary nature of his messages because he wanted to overthrow the entire foundations of the inherited Western thought by placing the necessity and autonomy of politics beyond good and evil; that is, beyond morality. Thus Machiavelli is presented as the "founder" of modern political theory.

The central theme of Joseph Tussman in *Obligation and the Body Politic* (New York: Oxford University Press, 1960) is that a theory of political obligation must be distinct from a theory of political behavior. An adequate theory of obligation, so Tussman argues, must be based on a system of agreements, which is a sophisticated version of the social-contract theory. To establish this system of agreements as an appropriate model for the body politic, a significant conception of the "common good," "right," "obligation and freedom under law," and "authority as distinguished from power" must be derived. Tussman also advances the idea that since obligation carries with it the notion of "ought," if such bases for the system of agreements, or more precisely, for obligation do not exist, the propriety of withdrawing membership from or even rebelling against civil society is not excluded. The book is rich with references to the insights of Plato and Hobbes.

In his edition of Thomas Hobbes's *De Cive or The Citizen* (New York: Appleton-Century-Crofts, Inc., 1949) Sterling P. Lamprecht regards this work as merely a preliminary draft of the exposition later immortalized in the *Leviathan*. The analysis is informative and valuable, though four chapters have been omitted, and passages of Hobbes's Latinized and unidiomatic English are likely to prove unintelligible to readers unfamiliar with Latin constructions. He also makes a succinct but critical differentiation between "Hǫbbism" and Hobbes's actual philosophy.

As noted earlier, given ample evidence that there is not only a Hobbes and Hobbism, but, *pari passu*, a Locke and Lockism, it would be remiss merely to conclude that the fable of Hobbes's absolutist antilibertarianism is matched by the myth of Locke's democratic libertarianism. It also seems to follow that, in spite of extensive commentary upon Hobbes and Locke, especially in the recent years, further research clearly is warranted. It should prove valuable to begin with an examination of Locke's correspondence and journals, especially during the years of his association with Lord Ashley. By illuminating the background of the development of Locke's political theory, the extent of Locke's oligarchic posture could be explicated. This is similar to Philip Abrams's approach to the theme of "conservatism" in his recent *John Locke: Two Tracts on Government* (London, Cambridge: Oxford University Press, 1967). The *Tracts*, written in 1660 and suppressed by Locke, seem little other than defences of nonresponsive government directed to stifling criticism from below. Accordingly, Abrams was concerned primarily with the freedoms of thought and expression and focused attention upon Locke's later works: *Essays on the Law of Nature, Essay Concerning Human Understanding, An Essay Concerning Toleration, Letters Concerning Toleration* and *The Reasonableness of Christianity*. The projected study would differ by relating a theme of oligarchy to *Locke's Two Treatises of Government*.

There is a strong possibility that considerably less difference exists between the "Constitutions" and the *Treatises* than previous scholars, including that super sleuth, Peter Laslett, have supposed. This seems a sound conclusion following from seemingly oligarchic tenets of the *Second Treatise*. First, even if the question of whether Locke held that men possessed inalienable rights is put aside, the version of rights in the *Second Treatise* concerns government only with the protection of life, liberty and property, not with life, liberty and the pursuit of happiness, unless the protection of prop-

erty is tantamount to happiness. That Locke insisted government
is concerned first and foremost with the increase of lands and the
right to employment of them rather than being concerned primarily
with producing conditions favorable to happiness seems to offer
further verification of his willingness to limit happiness to mean
the enjoyment and protection of material possessions. This would
also explain why Locke never used the word happiness to elucidate
his own position in the *Second Treatise*.

Second, Locke's apparent inequalitarian position not only casts
doubt upon the inalienability of men's rights, but certainly results
in a form of government that is to a profound degree independent
of a majority of society. Whether it be government characterized
by a prince's prerogative as a "moderated monarchy," or government by a select few as in "oligarchy," it is apparent that some
one or few possess attributes of superior significance sufficient to
rightly claim ruling powers. Seemingly, the theme of property determines the character of both fundamental tenets: the restrictive
sphere of rights and the form of government. Although unquestionably the *Second Treatise* is far less oligarchic than the "Constitutions," it appears more oligarchic than democratic in form and
tone. And on this basis it is closer to the "Constitutions" than
previously supposed.

A second direction of the proposed study encompasses the similarities between Hobbes and Locke. In this vein it would seem
valuable to examine Locke's papers written during the period when
John Edwards, one of Locke's critics bent on proving him a
Hobbesist, suggested that he had plagiarized from *Leviathan*.
Locke's reply in *A Second Vindication of the Reasonableness of
Christianity* is a rhetorical masterpiece which implies, without actually saying so, that he had never read *Leviathan*. At that time, of
course, Locke had possessed a personal copy of it for years; and of
equal interest, no less than five volumes in his personal library were
commentaries on it.

Laslett found it remarkable that while Locke's notebooks consisted largely of citations from the work of others, and although

they were meticulously referenced and arranged, not one reference or extract from Hobbes's works has been found in them. Perhaps this is not remarkable at all, especially if Edwards was close to the truth. Given the lack of explicit evidence to the contrary plus the absence of references to Hobbes in the notebooks, however, Laslett dismissed this possibility, accepted Locke at his word, and concluded that there is no direct major source of Locke's thought.

Admittedly there are few explicit, hard facts to justify a contrary conclusion. At the same time, certain inferential "soft" facts at least justify further research for firm evidence. As in the case of Locke's library, another soft fact results from Laslett's own scholarly efforts. In this regard, Laslett pointed to two quotations written by Locke; one on the flyleaf of a volume in his library and the other in one of his notebooks. After noting that not one of the notebooks contains a reference to Hobbes, he observed that in the whole Lockean corpus, "Only one citation has so far come to light, and . . . even then the famous passage from *Leviathan* written there is given without its source, and might appear to the unwary reader to have been a sentiment written by Locke himself." Is it not significant that in the single instance where a passage that is irrefutably from Hobbes's *Leviathan* appears in Locke's hand, Locke suddenly lost his meticulousness and failed to cite the source? Considered in relation to the quotation from Locke's notebook, this fact takes on even greater significance.

The notebook citation was taken from Robert Filmer's *Observations concerning the original of Government, Upon Mr Hobs Leviathan*. Locke paraphrased Filmer:

> Hobbs
> With noe small content I read Mr Hobs booke De Cive & his Leviathan about the rights of Soveraignty wch noe man yt I know hath so amply & Judiciously handled. Filmore. Obser. preface:

What seems of further significance emerges with Professor Laslett's observation that "Locke shared with Filmer the traditional analysis of sovereignty," even though he "blandly ignore[d] Filmer's acute critique of mixed government. . . ." Awareness of this fact points to a similarity that lies within one of the greatest matters of difference between Hobbes and Locke—the matter of whether sovereignty ought to be or can be divided.

A major difference between Locke and Filmer on the one hand, and Hobbes on the other, involves the nature and extent of sovereign power. For Hobbes, the sovereign power in any commonwealth encompasses only those powers necessary to attain the ends of society: safety and happiness. By definition it did not contain any power to thwart those ends. When he spoke of absolute power, he meant absolute within this context: it was as great as men could make it. Since men could not contract away any of their inalienable rights, which we see in the form of safety and happiness as the ends of civil society, and since sovereignty is nothing other than the result of this transfer, all forms of government are limited forms possessing absolute power within their legitimate spheres.

Locke and Filmer, on the other hand, viewed sovereignty as truly absolute and operable in any and all spheres. Therefore Locke felt the need to divide sovereignty in hopes of checking it, thereby protecting men's alienable rights to life, liberty, and property. This also would serve to explain why Locke may not have held that men possessed inalienable rights. If sovereignty encompasses so much power that it is absolute, any attendant rights could not possibly be inalienable.

The basic difference seems to come to this: for Hobbes, the social contract both establishes sovereignty and posits men's inalienable rights, thereby limiting all forms of government; Locke, on the other hand, seems to view the social contract as granting absolute power to government. A second contract determines the form of government and limits, if at all, that absolute power. Therefore it was in part because Locke did share Filmer's analysis of sovereignty that he diverged from his critique of mixed government. Locke reasoned that if sovereignty is absolute, the only way to check it is through mixed government, that is, to divide it.

Hobbes previously had noted that sovereignty could be limited by "dividing" it. But he argued that to limit power in this manner not only limited it with respect to rights, it also limited it within its appropriate sphere. He believed, moreover, that limiting power in this manner ignored with tragic results the nature of sovereignty and of man. When a man or group of men possess sovereignty, he or they rule and others obey. Thus to divide power is to give it to the one *and* the few *and* the many, or to any two of the three. In other words, it is to give the final say to representatives of each, even though they represent conflicting interests. Hobbes argued that to function, the respective rulers must possess natures not of this world. Such a system was exactly what he had in mind when he insisted that the fault with commonwealths was not in men as they are the matter of them, but as they are their makers. To divide sovereignty was to ignore human nature, for mixed government was realized only at expense of creating factions with an ineluctable result of civil war.

In *Leviathan* Hobbes wrote

> that such government, is not government, but division of the Common-wealth into three Factions, and [they] call it mixt Monarchy; yet the truth is, that it is not one independent Common-wealth, but three independent Factions; nor one Representative Person, but three. In the Kingdome of God, there may be three Persons independent, without breach of unity in God that Reigneth; but where men Reign, that be subject to diversity of opinions, it cannot be so. And therefore if the King bear the person of the People, and the generall Assembly bear also the person of the People, and another Assembly bear the person of a Part of the People, they are not one Person, nor one Soveraign, but three Persons, and three Soveraigns.

Therefore he favored unmixed government of monarchic form and, as noted above, he hoped to attain limited government through what he believed was the only means possible—invisible hand.

It is obvious why Locke "blandly ignored" Filmer's critique of mixed government. He had little faith in Hobbes's belief that monarchy inherently would provide protection of the sphere of rights. And since he also seems to have had similar reservations about the other pure forms, he apparently accepted mixed government as a surer means of protecting the sphere of rights, in spite of its class divisions and even if at risk of civil war. It came to a point of choosing which was the lesser evil to attain a positive good. Whereas Hobbes believed it was possible to attain both stability and protection of rights, Locke seems to have believed stability was attained at the expense of rights, or vice versa, and chose the latter. Although their favored forms of government differed, they nevertheless chose them on the basis of a similar end—a hope to secure the rights of men.

When one considers the extensive similarities in the thought of Hobbes and Locke, Locke's obvious familiarity with *Leviathan*, and the absurdity of Locke's possessing five commentaries on a book he never or barely read, it appears that Edwards may have been at least correct in part. This is not to say that Locke cribbed from Hobbes, but rather that he may have been substantially influenced by him. That Hobbism was considered then, as now, absolutistic, atheistic, and maleficent could explain why Locke was so careful to avoid references to him. Since to be associated in any way risked anathema, a prudent man would take the necessary steps to avoid that connection.

Whereas this does not disprove Laslett's thesis that there is no major source of Locke's thought, it does suggest that if Hobbes were the major source it is not at all remarkable that Locke made no references to him. It suggests, furthermore, that the absence of such references does not constitute firm evidence that Hobbes was not one, if not *the*, major source of Locke's political thought.

In the light of all this, further study seems warranted to determine the extent to which Locke may be said to be obligarchic and the extent and nature of the similarities and dissimilarities in the political philosophies of Hobbes and Locke.

Index

mentioned, 10–14 passim; 103, 110, 112, 116

Democratic: society, xii; principles, 10; Hobbes's division of, 92; mentioned, 11, 12

Democratic-libertarian: Hobbes's theory, 121

Democratic-republic, 111

Demos, 22

De Tocqueville, Alexis. *See* Tocqueville, Alexis de

Diamond, Martin: Divine right, 6; difference between man and man, 33; *The Federalist*, 98; authoritative exposition, 99; mentioned, 11, 103, 114, 121

Domestic convulsion, 110

Duty and liberty of subjects, 82

Earl of Shaftsbury (Sir Anthony Ashley Cooper), 23

Economic: interests, 10; forces, 139

Economic determinism, 114

Edwards, John, 144, 145, 148

Egoism, psychological, xi, 3, 6, 44, 114

Elites, 6

End, 40

Epistola de Tolerantia, Locke, 25

Equal, 8, 15

Equalitarian, Hobbes, 43

Equalitarianism: modern approach, 21; mentioned, 7, 21, 47, 48

Equality: all men are created equal, 21; proportionate, 29; Declaration of Independence, 33; essential, 48; mentioned, 24

Erasmian, 25

Estate, 23

"&c": unnamed sources of the Declaration, 9–10

Execution, 17

Executive: Publius on, 115; tyranny, 115; mentioned, 20

Executive power, 18, 118

Exposition, authoritative, Martin Diamond, 99

External impediment: absence of, 72; artificial chains, 73–74; mentioned, 68–78 passim

Faction: definition of, 104; effects of, Publius, 104; curing mischiefs of, Publius, 105; sources of, 107; majority, 109–18 passim; minority,109; majority coalescence, 114

Faculties: men's, 106; man's diverse, 109

Fear: of death, 53; relating to liberty, 69; consistent with liberty, Hobbes, Pennock, 70; of aversion and hurt, 72; of the sovereign, 73; equated with danger in Pennock, 75

Federal Convention, 10

Federalist, The: Publius, x; Martin Diamond, 98; shortcomings, 101; republic of, 103; mentioned, 11, 100

Federalist Papers, 9

Feudal stage, absence of, 139

Filmer, Robert: differences with Locke, 146; views on sovereignty, 146; mentioned, 145

Waynesburg College Library
Waynesburg, Pa.   15370